The Leader's Inner Source

First published in 2023.

ISBN: 978-1-86922-566-7
eISBN: 978-1-86922-975-7

Published by KR Publishing
Tel: (011) 706-6009
E-mail: orders@knowres.co.za
Website: www.kr.co.za

Typesetting, layout and design: Cia Joubert, cia@knowres.co.za
Cover design: Marlene De Lorme, marlene@knowres.co.za
Ghostwriter: Elzet Blaauw, elzet@elzetblaauw.com
Editing and proofreading: Jennifer Renton, jenniferrenton@live.co.za
Project management: Cia Joubert, cia@knowres.co.za

The Leader's Inner Source

Engage your whole self to navigate chaos and complexity and make a meaningful impact

by
Rean du Plessis (PhD)

kr
publishing

2023

To the five young men in my life:

Lead the way

And to all the leaders who have walked with me

and whose collective wisdom I share here:

I am eternally grateful for each of you.

Table of Contents

❖

Acknowledgements

❖

I would like to thank the following people who contributed to my thinking and growth as a person and a leader:

- My wife, Trudie, and our children, Jean, Michael, Hattingh, Zani and Micke. You and our growing family have taught me most about life and leadership.

- My spiritual leaders, mentors and friends:

    - Nevil Norden, Francois van Niekerk, the late Corrie van Heerden, Dr Chuck Day, Karl Landman, Elmo Lombard, Peet Bekker, Halima Daniels, Adele Vrey, Andrew Butters, Iain Shippey and Tshidi Nyama.

    - My weekly prayer partners, Dr Pieter Roos and Nico van Staden. I value that you walk with me on this spiritual journey and that you challenge me.

    - Key academic and business partners, colleagues, clients and friends who have supported, trusted, mentored and challenged me professionally and intellectually by demonstrating different aspects of life, leadership and leadership thinking during this journey: the late Dr David Hendry, Dolph Kruger, Andy Beytel, Henning Olivier, the late Peet Coetzee, Ben Spies, Prof Johan Coetzee, Russel Schwartz, Prof Ben Anderson, Dr Maretha Prinsloo, Nick Mannie, Nonhlanhla Mkhize, Mandla Nyirenda, Svenja Wachter, Mapi Mobwano, Ronaldt Mafoko, Indira Moudi, Jan van der Westhuizen, Nobantu Masebelanga, Howard John, Paul Ibona, Tjaart van der Walt, Andy Johnson, Simone Le Hane, Lovelle Henderson, Pat Roberts, Dale Hillary, Lindi Mkhondo, Magnus Karlberg, Les Weiss, Delani Mthembu, Clive Knobbs, Sundra Naidoo, Tumi Moloto, Louis Ferreira and Ivan Wayland.

- Thys Sabbagha, Brand Pretorius and Rassie Alberts, for living out the type of leadership that this book describes.

- The people who helped me shape this message into a book:

  ◦ Elzet Blaauw, for helping me find the right words and craft it into a book.

  ◦ Peet Bekker, for the diagrams.

  ◦ The 16 people who gave feedback as I was writing this book, including those who are not already mentioned above: Werner Meyer, Mark Arendse, Justice Nkosi, Joshua Bhengu and John Grobler.

- The 18 industry leaders who participated in my PhD study and contributed to the leadership framework.

- The 300+ executive leaders with whom I had the privilege to have coaching conversations over the last 19 years.

- Everyone who has contributed to my life.

Most importantly, I want to acknowledge the Spirit of God who inspired me to write this book.

About the author

❖

Dr Rean du Plessis (PhD) facilitates development and growth in executive leaders, their teams and their organisations.

In our disruptive and uncertain world, leaders must find clarity and maintain focus to achieve results.

To deliver lasting business results, leaders need self-insight. They must understand their own potential and how to develop it. They need to know how to harness and grow their influence, especially on an executive and board level.

Leaders also need to know how to bring out the potential in their teams and keep them engaged. They must be able to create an organisational culture in which people can be safe and well, as well as able to adapt to changing conditions while delivering business results.

Rean assists executive leaders and their organisations to:

- challenge their thinking and gain clarity and focus;
- navigate career transitions;
- improve engagement;
- create high-performance cultures;
- grow and develop up-and-coming leaders; and
- create more spiritual awareness.

From his background and experience as an executive coach, facilitator and organisational psychologist, Rean employs a wide range of methods tailored to his clients' needs, including:

- one-on-one leadership coaching;

- team alignment and strategy;

- group coaching and facilitation; and

- research and assessments.

He has worked with clients across the globe, including the United Kingdom, Saudi Arabia, Kenya, Ghana, Mozambique and Canada, in industries as varied as mining, oil, financial services, medical, telecommunications and manufacturing.

Rean is passionate about unleashing the thought-provoking processes that inspire the full development of the unique potential that lies within everyone.

He lives with his wife, Trudie, at Shelley Point on the West Coast of South Africa. They have five biological children, four more through marriage and one grandchild.

Contact Rean and his team at https://leadershipcoachingafrica. com/contact-us/ or email him at reanduplessis@rdup.com. To get on Rean's exclusive mailing list with content for former and current clients, contact him via email.

Introduction

❖

Where do we go for wisdom and guidance when information and experience cannot give us the right answers?

What source do we draw from if there are no data and information on the topic which requires our leadership? What is our reference point if we face a situation unlike anything we or, for that matter, anyone else in history has faced before? What if we cannot know what is true because others might be withholding or misrepresenting facts due to personal agendas?

How do we as leaders position ourselves and lead others in this context? Is there a place from where we can glean knowledge that lies outside the scope of our rational minds?

These are the questions which lie at the heart of this book.

Can you identify?

To illustrate these questions, consider the situations that the following three leaders find themselves in. Even though they are fictitious characters, they and their challenges are based on real people and situations.

Sibusiso is the Group CEO of a South African-based tele-communications corporation with an international footprint. Sibu is a values-driven person who is deeply committed to creating jobs and alleviating poverty in South Africa, however, he reports to a board and shareholders who only care about double-digit growth – at any cost.

How does he grow the corporation sustainably while staying true to his personal values?

Or consider Pratibha, a brilliant and dynamic global leader who is on a mission to end world hunger. I first met Pratibha a decade ago when she was in a corporate role at an oil and gas multinational. Since then, she has gone into business herself in the agriculture and food industry, which is clearly much more aligned with her passion.

From the outside, Pratibha is immensely successful. She is the president of a flourishing business that is aligned with her personal mission in life, and they have recently won a national award for their contribution to sustainability.

But Prathiba knows this is not the peak of her career. She sees the potential for global change that will truly make it possible to end world hunger. How does she break through political, ethnic and gender bias to get a seat at the table of global organisations like the United Nations and the World Bank to make the impact she is capable of?

Or, lastly, consider Hugo, one of the nicest people you will ever meet and a senior HR manager at a mining company. While Hugo is very quick to grasp strategic initiatives and drive results, he also truly cares about the people he works with.

He recently got promoted to a more strategic and less tactical role. He's excited about how quickly his career is progressing and making a bigger impact.

But a few months in, he feels as if he's floundering in the new role. For one, he has two people he reports into: a line head in mining and the corporate head of HR. Whenever he gets buy-in from one, the other has concerns, and vice versa. And they treat him completely differently depending on the context: in individual meetings, he's a trusted partner, but in corporate settings, he hardly gets acknowledged.

Hugo is struggling to make sense of the politics and to get anything done. He feels as if his career might be in jeopardy. How can he stay the nice person he is and navigate this political playground?

Our complex systemic reality

Whether you identify with Sibu, Prathiba or Hugo, as a leader in the twenty-first century, you have to navigate several complex challenges by default.

Globalisation, regional conflict and continuously new and emerging technologies have made our already complex, interwoven world even more complex and unpredictable. Leaders at all levels do not have the luxury of only leading their constituency in the context of their organisation, sector, industry, region or country. We are always navigating our position in the complex cosmic system of our twenty-first century world.

It is obvious that these are things someone like Sibu or Prathiba must take into consideration. They are leading on a national and international scale, after all. But even someone like Hugo must find a way through countless conflicting yet interconnected agendas, known and unknown, many far outside our sphere of influence. These conflicting forces influence our perception of reality and the sphere of our leadership directly and indirectly.

For instance, the head of HR might be ignoring Hugo because she was just informed that they would have to lay off several people in his division. She can't risk telling him yet because his line head in mining has not yet been informed. All of this will eventually affect Hugo, but in that moment, it is outside his sphere of knowledge or control.

To add another layer of complexity to it, consider what the reason for these layoffs could be. There might be international conflict between different world powers, such as what we've been seeing between the USA and Russia and China. If the USA has imposed sanctions against Russia and China, those countries might be getting rid of their surplus mining output in Africa. That is causing lower demand for the product of Hugo's division at the mining company, hence the layoffs.

All these forces are affecting Hugo's career. He needs to navigate his way not only through the complexity of his organisation's politics, but also through this complex global reality.

The term *global leader* is therefore no longer only applicable to leaders who are responsible for complex, international situations. It also does not extend only to leaders, who lead on a national level. These days, every leader must be a global one to navigate our interconnected global and cosmic reality. And what I have learned from my engagement with global leaders working in multiple systems is that creating a different future is a long-term process with milestones that are not always concrete and visible.

We are always part of a system, that is, a web of seen and unseen relationships. Our global system encompasses every aspect of life: ideological, geopolitical, economic, environmental, health, technological and religious.

This fast-shifting, interconnected global system constantly puts us as leaders in a position where we must actively create clarity and predictability. If we are not consciously navigating the system's changing waters, we end up simply being followers of a system that creates and dictates our future.

However, the reality is that we are not always able to be fully aware of what is happening on a global scale. And many events that influence us profoundly are beyond our control.

Black swans

This scenario has been our reality for the past few decades already, however, we are often unaware of its impact as change generally happens gradually. We become acutely aware of our interconnected, unpredictable global reality when we are confronted with a black swan event, such as the Covid-19 pandemic of 2020 and beyond.

Nassim Taleb coined the term *Black Swan* as part of his "Black Swan Theory" in the book by the same name, *The Black Swan: The Impact of the Highly Improbable*.[1] Black swans are unexpected events of large magnitude and consequence that play a dominant role in history. Such events, considered extreme outliers, collectively play vastly larger roles than regular occurrences. Black swans reveal systemic weaknesses. They also show us just how dependent we are on a system over which we have very little control; much less than we would like to admit.

Let me be clear: it is not the actual black swan event which we must navigate, though that is often what we end up doing reactively. The black swan simply makes underlying realities explicit and often causes a systemic shift in our perceived reality. If it is not one event, another would have exposed the systemic weaknesses and dependencies which we were unaware of before.

We cannot prepare for everything.

For example, Covid-19 was recognised as a global pandemic in the first quarter of 2020 when the healthcare systems of country after country was not able to deal with its impact. Large numbers of people died because we were ill-prepared for such an off-the-charts event.

Governments across the world did not know what to do. In an unprecedented move, they shut down our societies to contain the spread of the disease until the healthcare system could ready itself.

However, as we now know, the globally interdependent economies of the world were ill-prepared to handle such a shutdown of activity. As I am writing to you in 2023, we are still suffering economically and socially from the decisions made during the pandemic – and we might be for years still.

Covid-19 tested leaders' abilities to make complex decisions about economic policy, social welfare and environmental sustainability.

The tough part is that the right thing to do in a situation like this is not apparent. It's easy to think that the right course of action in a complex situation like this is obvious. However, we as leaders regularly overestimate our ability to understand our position and the realities we face.

If the right thing to do at the breakout of the Covid-19 pandemic had been obvious, every government would have done it, and there would not have been so much contention over what the correct course of action was. So much was still unknown at this stage that what was true or not was not yet clear.

As humans, we like to see a person with an opposite view than ours as being wrong or motivated by ulterior motives. The truth is that most people do what they believe is right. It is merely that our beliefs about right and wrong conflict with many others' beliefs.

Every person's views in life depend on the data they have access to, how they interpret that data and how they apply the information collected to a given situation. All of that is based on their values, ideas and views of how the world works and should work, which is all shaped by what they have encountered in life. Those variables differ for each person.

In addition to our own values, all of us, including the most senior leaders in the world, are at the mercy of the interpretations and decisions made by others. Those others, like us, are acting based on their limited views. They believe in their own stories, egos and personal agendas – over which we have no or, at most, very little control.

In the example of Covid-19, each country's most senior political leaders made decisions of how to react to Covid-19 in consultation with experts and to the best of their ability. However, they were also impacted by the decisions made by other countries' leaders, which, for the most, were entirely outside their control.

As leaders, we thrive on the predictable and controllable. We are lulled into complacency by the fact that we have access to knowledge and data unlike ever before in human history. We feel powerful because we think we can make informed decisions unlike ever before. We rely on the analytical and strategic ability of our rational minds, those of our advisors and consultants, and those of the computational powers of the powerful technologies we have access to. However, some of these analytic approaches are founded on linear and mechanical methods that undermine the complex human element of our existence.

During and following a black swan event, we are left without those luxuries. By definition, a black swan is unpredictable. If you were ready for a black swan event before it hit, it was due to providence, not skill. If we can prepare for it, it would not be a black swan event anymore. We cannot anticipate it, so we cannot prepare for it – at least not in the way we would for the highly predictive reality we tend to focus on as leaders.

In preparation for, during and after a black swan event, we also cannot determine our course ahead based on analytical and strategic thinking alone; we need to forge a new way forward. We need more than our knowledge and rational insight, which is based on past events, to get us there. The ability to work across agendas and recognise our interconnectedness globally and beyond is more urgent than ever.

Lack of engagement

If we as leaders are overwhelmed by our complex systemic reality, the people we are leading are even more so.

They are also part of the bigger cosmos that we as leaders are navigating. However, they are often at the mercy of how their leaders choose to navigate that reality on their behalf, whether they agree with it or not. And often, they do not even benefit from the course of action chosen on their behalf.

The 2023 Edelman Trust Barometer shows that trust in government and business leaders decreased from the previous year and that the general sentiment towards both these groups are distrust rather than trust.s.[2]

The 23 years of the Edelman Trust Barometer's existence has been marked by cycles of distrust in government, business, the media and NGOs. Back in 2009, the Edelman Trust Barometer found that "fewer than one in five people trust corporate or government leaders to tell the truth when confronted with a difficult issue".[3]

The effect of this lack of trust is alarmingly low engagement levels at work and in other spheres of society. The statistics on engagement at work is especially frightening. Research conducted by Gallup indicated that 60% of people are emotionally detached at work and 19% are miserable.[4]

Another study published in the *Harvard Business Review* found that more than nine out of ten employees "are willing to trade a percentage of their lifetime earnings for greater meaning at work". As they put it very bluntly in the article, "Across age and salary groups, workers want meaningful work badly enough that they're willing to pay for it".[5]

And yes, disengagement is really a problem. Only 21% of employees in 2022 were engaged.[6] That means that only one in five employees show the following patterns of behaviour:[7]

- They don't often let problems become an excuse for inaction or destroy their ability to perform.

- They focus on their strengths.

- They are intentional about engagement.

- They take accountability for their performance instead of blaming others when things don't go as they want it.

Compared with people at low-trust companies[8], people at high-trust companies report 74% less stress, 106% more energy at work, 50% higher productivity, 13% fewer sick days, 76% more engagement, 29% more satisfaction with their lives and 40% less burnout.

Leaders have understood the stakes of a lack of trust and resulting disengagement for a while now. In its 2016 global CEO survey, PWC reported that 55% of CEOs think that a lack of trust is a threat to their organisation's growth. They are right. Business units with engaged workers have 23% higher profit compared with those with miserable workers.[9]

How do we as leaders create an environment of trust and change the status quo of disengagement in our sphere of leadership?

How do we facilitate an environment where employees find meaning in what they do? How do we create spaces where people feel safe enough to contribute to the creation of the type of organisations, cities and countries we need to succeed in our day and age? How do we make these spaces of collaboration and partnership a higher priority?

Providing a convincing argument for engagement or enticing everyone on your team to attend another training programme on engagement is not enough, though there is a place for those tools. People do not engage with their heads – they engage with their hearts. Going through the motions and jumping through the hoops is not enough to get real results.

We need a different type of leadership. We need a different kind of leader.

Re-examining the role of the leader

To lead in the context of the challenges that we face in our world and our workplaces, we as leaders need to return to certain fundamental questions about life and therefore leadership.

- Who am I and who am I leading?

- How do I view other people?

- Why do I do what I do? What drives me?

- How can I be my best self – all I was meant to be?

- How can I make a meaningful contribution?

- How will I contribute to the future – in other words, what legacy will I leave?

We need to ask ourselves these questions as individuals and as leaders. We need to ask how we are going to engage with those questions and how we are going to allow those we lead to engage with them. Amid all the information overload, we must decide what counts and what does not.

To answer these questions, we need to extend ourselves beyond our rational thinking and use intuition. We need to engage our whole selves.

Why do we really think what we think and do what we do? What do we believe in and value, and what is the foundation of our values and principles?

Otto Scharmer, the author of *Theory U*, says that we know a great deal about leaders, their decision-making, what they do and how they do it, "but, we know very little about the 'inner place'... the source from which [leaders] operate".[10]

What "inner source" does the leader go to for wisdom and guidance in making decisions on an unconscious level when they do not know or do not have enough information? We have all experienced moments where we felt a presence, a wow moment, synchronicity or some influence outside ourselves. Do we know how to tap into that latent source inside us when our analytical minds and strategic abilities fail us?

And how do we engage with those we lead – only with our heads or also at a deeper level? Can we engage with others from that special place inside ourselves and allow them the space to do the same?

Unleashing the leader's whole self

The challenges faced by the global leader outlined above and the questions that they ask of leadership were the instigators that led to my PhD study.[11] As an executive coach and organisational psychologist, I come across these challenges and questions again and again. My PhD research focused on understanding the challenges and finding ways to address them.

As part of my study, I engaged with several leaders to determine what type of person a leader needs to be to achieve sustainable business results in our current global reality. My study investigated the role of the corporate leader's spiritual self in achieving sustainable business results. It sought to get an in-depth understanding of leaders' inner source – what resources do they access and rely on beyond the cognitive and emotional level?

Based on the interviews I conducted and by incorporating previous leadership research, seven dimensions emerged as keys to effective, holistic leadership. Together, these seven dimensions provide a leadership framework of how leaders can achieve sustainable business results by engaging their whole selves as well as those of their employees and stakeholders.

THE LEADER'S INNER SOURCE

SYSTEMIC CONTEXT

④ CLARITY OF DIRECTION

⑥ HUMANE CONNECTIVITY
Appreciating one's own and others' intrinsic value

⑤ 'Detaching' from the vision and focusing on being optimal now

UNCONDITIONAL ENGAGEMENT
with the person, trusting, moving forward

SPIRITUAL AWARENESS
Becoming aware of a spiritual dimension and the spiritual self ⑦

RELATIONSHIPS (horizontal oval)

CREATING INFINITE POSSIBILITIES
③ Appreciating the unlimited nature of potential

INSPIRED CREATIVITY
② Being inspired to inspire

POTENTIAL (vertical oval)

MINDFULNESS
① Journey to find our Self and our Source

SUSTAINABLE RESULTS

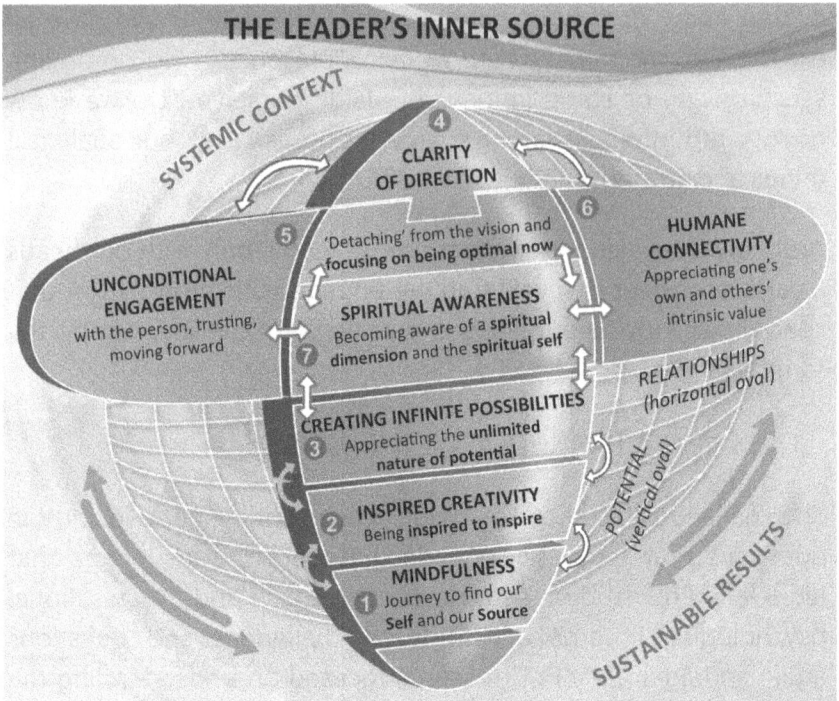

I chose to refer to the "global leader" because any leader in our age navigates global realities, whether they acknowledge that they do or not, as mentioned already. I used the word "spirit" to refer to that deepest part of each of us, the "inner place" Otto Scharmer refers to. Lastly, "sustainable business results" include much more than organisational growth and profit.

The vertical oval of the framework includes the four dimensions that relate to the leader's drive to unleash their full potential. These four dimensions are mindfulness, inspired creativity, creating infinite possibilities and clarity of direction. Each of the dimensions stacks on top of each other because they build on each other.

The horizontal oval of the framework includes the two dimensions which relate to the leader's drive to connect with others through relationships. The two dimensions in this oval are unconditional engagement and humane connectivity. These dimensions support the final dimension of the vertical oval, which is clarity of direction.

The last and seventh dimension lies at the heart of the framework where the two ovals intersect. This dimension is spiritual awareness. Spiritual awareness is the source from which all the other dimensions feed and vice versa.

In the years since I have completed my study, I have tested these concepts daily in practical leadership contexts. I have seen these concepts play out in the lives of leaders like Sibu, Prathiba and Hugo. It is the great need of leaders like these for these concepts combined with a deep inner drive that have prompted me to write this book.

It is clear to me and many other leaders that there is an opportunity to lead differently, which is precisely what is offered by the framework that emerged from my research.

In the chapters that follow, I elaborate on each of the dimensions of this framework in more detail. I explain what they are, why they are important and how they are practiced by leaders. I also show how they relate to each other and work together to produce sustainable results, in business as well as other spheres of society.

The potential of a different kind of leadership

I started this introduction by focusing on the challenges that global leaders face today. It is certainly not where I want to end it. The leadership framework that emerged from my research is not one that leaders revert to in the face of mounting challenges. It is one that leaders can choose to rise to.

The dimensions that my research uncovered are not new ones. They are characteristic of many of the most successful leaders in all eras of the history of humankind.

During the past century or two, many of these dimensions have been practiced less often. They have been perceived as unfashionable or even inappropriate in a society that has become increasingly selfish. They have often been downplayed in leadership, especially in the corporate context.

These dimensions never completely disappeared from successful leadership practice, however. During the past few decades especially, there has been a turn towards leadership that is more humane. Many visionary leaders are rediscovering the importance of these dimensions; my study simply highlighted what is already happening and delivering impressive results.

To end this introduction, I invite you: dare to entertain the idea of a different kind of leadership than what most of us think of when we hear the word.

Imagine what your organisation would be like if everyone, including yourself, comes to work fully engaged and with high levels of trust and energy. Think what the world could look like if organisations truly function to make it a better place.

It might sound idealistic to you, impossible even. It does not have to be. I have witnessed and experienced it. This book offers you the tools to experience it too, in your own life, organisation and leadership.

I am not saying that it will be easy. These dimensions are not a panacea or a quick fix to a difficult situation. They are beacons to guide us on our leadership journey.

Whether you're an upcoming or an established leader, these dimensions are there to remind us that there is more for us to do and be as leaders.

Questions for reflection

Before you proceed with the rest of this book, I'd encourage you, as I would any coaching client, to reflect on some questions.

Each chapter of this book will conclude with such a list of questions.

Reflection is not always an easy exercise, but honestly engaging with these questions will greatly help you integrate and apply this knowledge to get real benefit from this book.

Consider using a notebook and pen to write down what these questions prompt for you. Write down your thoughts and feelings in response to each question using the simplest words you can. Many people find that exercises like these are easier to do by hand than by typing.

If you have a coach or a closed loved one with whom you share things like this, I encourage you to have a conversation about your reflection, too.

- How intentional am I about making time to reflect on a deeper level about how I live and lead?

- Am I willing to examine what my 'inner source' means for me?

- Do I see an opportunity to develop myself even further as a leader?

- How willing am I to invest the time and energy as well as be intentional about growing myself as a leader?

- To what extent have I surrounded myself with mentors and coaches to support my growth as a 'different' kind of leader who fully accesses my 'inner source'?

THE LEADER'S CONTEXT

❖

Before we delve into the seven dimensions of the leadership framework, I want to spend some more time on the context in which this leadership framework is practiced. Chapter 1 therefore focuses on the external context of our complex, systemic world, while Chapter 2 reflects on the leader's self.

This section is fairly theoretical. It explains how to understand concepts rather than focusing on real-world applications.

I prefer to get a conceptual grasp of the context before I get practical. If that's not your style, please don't get bogged down in abstract concepts. What's important is applying what you learn and forming leadership practices that work for you.

If you are someone who prefers practical application over abstract theory, feel free to skip forward to Chapter 3. From there onwards, we get very practical.

If you skip ahead, I do advise that you take note of what is covered in Chapter 1 and 2. As you encounter concepts in later chapters, you might also want to return to this section to clarify what they mean and therefore apply them better.

Chapter 1

The leader's external reality

❖

As leaders in the twenty-first century, we function in a reality that's different than, say, 50 years ago.

We all know that, however, because we know our reality experientially, it is not always easy to distance ourselves from it to truly grasp what that means. It's very easy to slip into the belief that *of course* something is right or wrong – the preferred course of action or not.

The thing is, in 20 or 30 years, in hindsight it might be very obvious that the assumptions we now hold are not as obviously right. Our known reality might become illuminated by some new information that we do not yet have.

Because we only know in part, I believe it's helpful to hold up the mirror of theory to remind us of what our society believes and why we function as we do. This chapter offers some theories and principles to help us think about and engage with the complex, cosmic systemic reality in which we as leaders operate.

The challenge of consumerism

In most of the world, capitalism has triumphed over the other extreme of the economic spectrum: communism. Even in the few remaining communist states like China, more and more elements of capitalism have been introduced to ensure a flourishing economy.

In a capitalist society, trade and industry are controlled by private and public ownership operating for profit. In its opposite, a communist society, the state is in control, and it distributes resources to all citizens, with less emphasis on the value of their input.

One of the main drawbacks of communism is that it stymies private initiative. Capitalism gives individuals freedom to decide what they value and what the market should offer, which is a strong catalyst for progress. It is why it is the economic system that has triumphed over every other economic paradigm so far.

Our challenge is that capitalism has evolved into short-sighted consumerism. The consumerist system treats humans as an adjustable variable, and it casts us in the role of only acting in our short-term selfish interests.

Because "what is in it for me" is a key driver of our behaviour in consumerism, people make choices based on what feels good in the moment, without regard for the long-term results for themselves or others. Corporate business in a consumerist society values profits at the cost of people and the environment. It works for a few at the expense of most others.

Consumerism is not sustainable or healthy on several levels. It is not good for us, future generations or the planet. Many people realise it. It has resulted in the rise of environmental, social and governance (ESG) initiatives backed by the support of government and investors.

However, at many organisations, ESG initiatives are still mostly a tick box or a plaster. For instance, in early 2023, the multinational corporation Shell was sued for "greenwashing", or giving investors and regulators the false impression that it was addressing its negative impact on the climate, when in fact it was not.

It's easy to point the finger at Shell, and yet we all benefit from the energy that these companies generate. The path out of consumerism is not as simple as implementing an ESG initiative or two.

The challenge we face as leaders on all levels of society is how do we ensure sustainable use of the natural resources under our control? To add to the challenge, how do we create and distribute wealth in a sustainable manner at the same time?

Yes, as leaders we know that those are the questions our generation is asking, however we are faced with more than a theoretical questions. Our capitalist, consumerist society asks us and our organisations to produce value in the form of growth and profits, while at the same time overcoming its limitations. We have to solve the problem in practice before anyone has found the answer.

Because several of my clients over the years have been in industries like mining, oil and gas, and agriculture and food production, I have seen many strong leaders struggle with how to balance shareholder expectations for growth with shifting public expectations around sustainability.

As much as these leaders personally care about sustainability, the success of their careers is dictated by growth and profitability. I can imagine that leaders without a very firm moral compass can easily succumb to solutions that are ethically dubious

The resolution of this tension is by no means easy or simplistic.

For instance, consider Prathiba's company in the agriculture and food production sector. Yes, the company has won sustainability awards, yet they simultaneously have to grapple with a shrinking user base because environmental awareness is causing the public to consume less of their core product in favour of greener alternatives.

Because I know Prathiba, I know her company pursues sustainability because it's the right thing to do. However, even if she didn't believe in it, it would have made economic sense to do it to give them the edge in an increasingly competitive market. In these circumstances, it's very easy for leaders without firm convictions to simply tick boxes instead of truly grappling with this tension and living true to higher values.

The challenge of a secular business environment

Let's consider another assumption of our external reality that's not always made explicit.

In most spheres of society, especially in the Western world, it is acceptable and respectable practice to maintain a strict split between the sacred and secular, our public and private lives, business and the spiritual.

Talking about our faith and spirituality at work, or in other public contexts such as school or government, is frowned upon. In most parts of the world, we are allowed spiritual freedom, but we must practice it privately at home or in a church, temple or mosque. It must be kept separate from business, government and even charitable or developmental endeavours.

The challenge with this strict split between the sacred and secular is that our reality is interconnected. We cannot simply leave a part of our being at home; it is part of who we are. We cannot deny it and remain authentic. And because it is part of us, it is also part of our organisations.

Most of us as individuals believe in the importance of people, the planet and many other matters of principle. However, we function in organisations that often do not uphold those same values. By values, I do not mean the words stuck up on the walls of our buildings. Advertised values are the standards by which we are expected to operate. Actual values are evidenced in what we do every day under pressure; they are seen in our decisions and actions. That is what we really value.

The result of this conflict in values is a person who operates in an organisation with an essence that is very different from that of the person. What I call the corporate soul of the organisation is often in direct conflict with the spiritual self of its employees and leaders.

The instinct of the leader who is faced with such challenges with no clear-cut answers is to seek the answer in the short term, the concrete, and what has worked in the past. Unfortunately, although rational thinking got us far, the challenges we now face need answers that extend beyond our rational capability. More and more leaders are aware of a spiritual dimension, and some are seeking out spiritual answers to the challenges that they face.

Among our three characters, both Prathiba and Sibu consider themselves to be spiritual people. Even though Prathiba and I do not share the same religion, at the end of a coaching session, she has asked me more than once to pray for her. I first met Sibu in a religious context, not through work. Our initial connection came from our strong belief in living out our spiritual values through our work.

However, even while leaders such as Prathiba and Sibu might find solace in their private spirituality, the secular business environment does not readily offer a platform for them to share what they have gained privately. It is incredibly challenging to live out our deepest beliefs and values in our daily work. As a result, our organisations and the world as a whole are worse off because of it.

I have witnessed this challenge most acutely in Sibu's career. I have the highest admiration for how he navigates morally challenging situations and expectations without sacrificing his deepest-held beliefs. But I have also heard him admit, "My hands are tied here", for instance when contractual obligations are requiring the morally inferior scenario.

And, most tellingly, Sibu is very careful how he speaks about his spiritual beliefs at work. While people love to extoll the mantra that we should bring "our whole self to work", even a perceivedly powerful group CEO like Sibu doesn't feel as if he can.

The challenge of distrust and disengagement

Based on the consequences of consumerism and secularism, the challenge of distrust and disengagement that I touched on in the introduction is no surprise.

The world is becoming aware of the shortcomings of our consumerist society. People are looking to their leaders in all spheres of society to find a better way of doing business and life. Leaders themselves are aware that the system in which they operate often conflicts with their personal and spiritual beliefs and values. The tentative answers surfacing from deep inside themselves, however, are not only rational – they are emotive, personal and spiritual.

Unfortunately, the secular workplace makes it extremely difficult for leaders to bring these untested, often tentative answers to the table as a means to forge a new way forward. Most often, leaders revert to the status quo of safety and continue with business as usual. It is predictable and personally lucrative.

Recently, at the start of the Covid-19 crisis when large parts of society were shut down by the government, a senior leader in a business told me that he immediately took action to reduce his costs. A major strategy included retrenchments which allowed the business to break even at the end of that same month. "At least I can sleep now," he commented. "And the people?" I wondered out loud. I was told that six weeks after that decision, they were still waiting for their unemployment insurance fund payments.

This leader is not a bad person. He is someone who cares about people in his daily life. However, faced with a difficult decision under pressure, he focused on the business and did not also keep the people in mind. What kept him awake at night was whether the business would make money or not, not whether his employees would have food to feed their families. The values of the organisation and the system in which it operates – to make a profit by any legal means – triumphed over the leader's personal values.

Another example comes from a highly respected and very successful business leader. He told me in private that he finds it extremely difficult to reconcile the expectations of double-digit growth held by his company's shareholders and his personal values of spending time with his family. When he must choose between the two, he usually picks the business over his family.

Followers notice these things. Their leaders proclaim lofty values, but when push comes to shove, they do not challenge the status quo. Too often, they choose short-term profit, easy re-election, selfish gain and the certainty of that pay check or bonus at the end of the year. That is why people stop trusting their leaders to do what is right and best for all. They disengage at work and from participating in society.

I must say that I have also noticed exceptions to this trend. During the technical recession of 2022, one company's executive team made the decision to sizably cut their own salaries to delay layoffs as long as possible. During Covid-19, one of my suppliers gave all their clients a three-month break in paying our monthly subscriptions. The loyalty that generous and unselfish gestures like these elicits is foreign to most of the business world these days.

Finding a sustainable alternative

It's easy for each person to point to another person or group of people as the source of a problem. It has become a favourite way for politicians to get elected.

The problem is that this strategy does not solve any problems. Furthermore, it is an indulgence that no true leader can afford.

Even if a leader is not responsible, leaders are always accountable for the system in which they operate. It is the leader's duty to design and create a desired environment and outcome. Finding a solution to the challenges above starts when the leader takes up that accountability.

The next step seems contradictory to the first: that the leader acknowledges that they do not have full control.

The reality in which we operate, whether we like it or not and whether we acknowledge it or not, is a complex, interconnected, global and cosmic system. Unlike the hierarchies we are so fond of creating in our organisations, a system has no single point of highest authority. No one actor has the final say over everyone and everything else. There is no final say and no ultimate control.

Even though you might think of yourself as that point of highest authority and control in your team, department or organisation, the truth is that it is not the whole truth. You are part of a bigger system, and the people "underneath" you (as we like to conceptualise it) are also parts of many other interconnected systems.

This truth is something that many upcoming leaders, like Hugo, struggle with. As individual contributors, they got results by taking control and exercising authority. As they grow into more strategic roles with higher complexity, this approach starts being a liability rather than an asset.

I have seen few people grow as much in this regard as Prathiba. When I met her a decade ago, she was a very competent individual contributor. As she progressed in her corporate career and then in leading her own company, I have seen how her awareness of complexity made her more people-orientated and interdependent.

It's this ability that has brought her to the cusp of making a truly global impact. She used to be the person who kicked open any doors – or walls – that were in her way. This past decade she has learnt that she needs to build a network upon which she can rely to open these doors for her.

As much as leaders must realise they're not in control, truly great leaders still take up accountability. Sibu is again someone that I admire immensely in this regard. When a certain strategic project didn't materialise the way that they had hoped, the company had to lay off some staff. Sibu took full responsibility for the call and the layoff notice came from him, not an HR messenger.

What's more, it wasn't simply a business decision for him. He personally felt the weight of leaving several households without a breadwinner. He mentioned to me that allowing himself to feel these emotions is the best way he's found to offset his personal propensity to take strategic risks.

When he makes these decisions, he weighs up the potential downside to the people involved, like layoffs, against the upside of success, in this case, many more employment opportunities. While he can't control all the variables that will result in success or failure, he takes full accountability for being the one that initiated these events, including when the outcomes are even more negative than what he or his team could have anticipated.

If you can come to terms with the fact that you are accountable without having control, you have come a long way in becoming a great leader.

Systems thinking

Systems thinking offers a useful alternative for us as leaders to think about our reality. Systems thinking is a holistic approach that focuses on the way that the combined parts of a management system interrelate and how management systems work over time and in the context of larger systems.

The systems thinking approach breaks away from traditional analysis which studies systems by breaking them down into their separate elements. Systemic problems are interconnected and interdependent; the major problems of our time cannot be understood in isolation.

Systems exist the way they do for a reason. They are usually not created out of nothing but evolve over time, and not always according to a coherent logic. Systems therefore have their uses but also their limitations. If certain conditions which allowed a system to function change, that system will either break or evolve into a system which caters for the new conditions.

Think, for example, of the 2008 financial crisis and the ensuing recession that swept across the world. As I am finalising this chapter, the aftermath of the Covid-19 pandemic is continuing to have a systemic impact in all spheres of society. Problems in one system – banking and health care, in these two examples – caused repercussions across many other systems that were intimately related to them, even though we were not aware of these relationships before the crisis hit.

Systems thinking as a way of leadership

The number of non-linear and unknown variables in a complex system forces leaders to operate in an environment of complexity and chaos. Systems thinking offers a way for leaders to think about and engage with this reality.

The authors Squires, Wade, Dominick and Gelosh describe systems thinking as the ability to think abstractly to:[12]

- incorporate multiple perspectives;
- work within a space where the boundary or scope of problem or system may be "fuzzy";
- understand the diverse operational contexts of the system;

- identify inter- and intrarelationships and dependencies;
- understand complex system behaviour, and most important of all; and
- reliably predict the impact of change to the system.

Without systems thinking, leaders tasked with managing a complex situation often make one of these crucial mistakes:

1. They tend to think that they take the whole system into account, but any single person will almost always fail to do so.
2. They usually do not consider all possible relationships.
3. They often fail to integrate after breaking the system into what they think are "manageable" parts.
4. They fail to recognise that the system extends beyond the physical realm, a fact that is seldom acknowledged.

Leaders must become more aware of the intricacies of systems and what lies beyond our known systems to overcome these common pitfalls.

Complexity and chaos as a given

As the number of unknown variables in our world increases, so do complexity and chaos. As humans and as leaders, we can shift a system from chaos and complexity to order and maintain it there so that our world is more predictable, with an adequate amount of effort and drive. However, that state of order and predictability will only last as long as there is no change[13] and as long as you invest enough energy. Any system left alone will tend to chaos naturally; it is the fundamental law of entropy in physics, and it applies to all facets of life.

A small percentage of people, around 5%, have the capacity to deal with many variables over an extended timeframe, as is needed for complex national and international leadership roles.[14] They can see the way forward through complexity and chaos, even over long time spans. Integration comes naturally to them. They can work with the whole and see into the future with clarity. The top 1% of these people are the leaders who are creating our future societies.

Not all leaders will have these levels of cognitive capacity – even though we can increase our cognitive ability in this regard by being very intentional about it. Those leaders who do have this innate ability have the huge responsibility to use it not only for their own benefit, but for those of others too. However, all leaders need to become comfortable with the fact that complexity and chaos are states that our world will revert to repeatedly – and which we as leaders will therefore need to deal with repeatedly.

Dealing with change during situations of chaos requires us to be attuned to the situation, listen carefully, start with what we know, make a decision using the information available to us, take action, let go and trust for a positive outcome. As we get systemic feedback from the impact of our decision, we constantly need to review the situation and go through the process again.

Integrate instead of divide

Leaders are generally known to divide and conquer. Departments are often called "divisions". Work is broken up into manageable pieces and dished out to those departments to execute.

The first problem comes when leaders must put these pieces together again. Secondly, as soon as something changes, all those pieces do not fit together so neatly anymore. Most people are focused on the short-term – what they can see now. They do not take a helicopter view of the situation. They are stuck in the maze and only look at the next wall that they can see.

Studies show that 85% of leaders test as reactive during competency assessments and only 15% are proactive.[15] Similarly, 85% of graduates only verify their assumptions and hypotheses when conducting research. Again, only 15% critically evaluate their hypotheses and beliefs or prove them false.[16] Kahneman's Nobel-prize-winning book *Thinking, Fast and Slow* similarly shows that many people who are well-qualified and in high-level jobs deal with unfamiliar information in a diagnostic manner, meaning they only confirm what there is.[17]

In Kahneman's more recent book, *Noise*[18], he and his co-authors state again that many of our conclusions are drawn from judgments whose true answer is unknown or even unknowable. Judgement is difficult because the world is a complicated and uncertain place. Almost all judgements are partly subjective, however, organisations operate expecting systems that consistently deliver judgments.

This is why leaders cannot afford to fall into the 85% who simply react to what life throws at them and never adjust their ideas and beliefs. Instead of only confirming and maintaining current systems, we need to influence and create future systems. Systemically-oriented leaders integrate things after breaking them apart. They can work with the whole with a focus on the future.

By definition, the role of a leader involves oversight. It places them in the best position to make links between aspects which others might not be able to. They always remember that the important thing is the whole and not the part or even the sum of the parts, and they look for solutions to problems outside of the boxes that they and others have drawn to make life easier.

The power of relationships

Relationships offer one of the most powerful tools to ensure integration and not division.

A system consists of fractals. A fractal is "a rough or fragmented geometric shape that can be split into parts, each of which is (at least approximately) a reduced-size copy of the whole".[19]

Relationships are the fractals of organisations and societies. Our bigger systems are held together by, and reflect the quality of, the relationships they are made of. The nature of relationships in an organisation or community also reflects the nature of that system.

The mantra "people are our greatest asset" has become very popular over the past few decades. That mantra only conveys half the truth: it is the relationships between people that is its greatest asset as opposed to people only. Based on systems thinking, the role of leaders in paving the way towards an alternative sustainable future is to view, and therefore cultivate, relationships between people as the biggest asset of an organisation or group.

Following a systems-approach, leaders will also pay careful attention to the types of relationships that are cultivated between people. Is the system encouraging and resulting in kindness, accountability, personal growth, care and love? Or is it causing fear, lack of accountability, stagnation, distrust and hatred? Do the employees in a business care about its clients and vice versa? Are managers kind towards their employees?

The relationships in a system determine the nature of that system and what it produces. Even in situations of chaos, relationships – for example, business networks – can provide security and stability.

Feedback

Feedback is essential for a system to evolve and have influence.

A high-functioning system continually exchanges feedback among its parts to ensure that they remain closely aligned and focused on achieving the goal of the system. To achieve its goals more effectively, the system makes adjustments where any of the parts or activities seem weakened or misaligned.

Growing organisations, like individuals, requires openness to systemic feedback. Feedback is not always delivered personally either; it is found in the results of any action. Both so-called success and failure provide feedback all the same. Successful leaders learn from and use both success and failure to grow themselves and their organisations.

Open communication is crucial to ensure quality feedback. We can acknowledge others through open communication, or we can use communication to control others.

One of the characteristics of poor communication and thus poor feedback is manipulation by withholding information. I learned to identify this pattern while working with psychopaths in prison. Psychopaths thrive on their above-average ability to predict human behaviour. They abuse this information to stay one step ahead and manipulate others for their gain.

Sadly, I have often seen senior leaders employ this same strategy. Research has found that 12% of corporate senior leadership displays psychopathic traits, which means it's 12 times more common in this group than the general population.[20]

If we're going to improve the systems in which we function, we have to rise above this type of behaviour, even though it is common in leadership. We need to open up communication channels and improve feedback so that the system in which we function can improve.

C Northcote Parkinson said, "The void created by the failure to communicate is soon filled with poison, drivel and misrepresentation".[21] As leaders, we are responsible for filling that void with meaningful content.

Personal change

The interconnectedness of different parts of a leadership system means that to change an organisational system requires personal change.

When most people, leaders included, receive feedback, especially negative feedback, their first instinct is to look for the problem outside themselves. They want to fix a process, a procedure or another person. It is easy to spot the weakness in another person, but it is much harder to spot it in ourselves.

Unfortunately for us, systemic change does not work this way. If you receive feedback, your first response should be to turn inward. The only thing in a system over which you have full control is yourself. It is the best way to start. Be very honest with yourself and be willing to change yourself first. Only when leaders take responsibility for themselves first can they model and spread that change to all levels of the system.

Leading the change in a system starts with personal change. In the words of a manager who grasped this principle: "How did we ever think we can transform this place without being transformed?"[22]

Or, phrased in different words: "Individual transformation of employees [including leaders] is (at least) as important as any organisational transformation. Without it, the chances of any transformation succeeding are low. Without it, the chances of an organisation continuing to evolve to respond to new changes are almost non-existent."[23]

The leader's role

The type of leadership that we are discussing here clearly asks much more of a person than analytical abilities, strategic skills or managerial leadership competencies.

Leaders must hold values that extend far beyond financial gain, and they must live true to themselves with integrity yet humility. They must do what they preach and preach what they do.

Their decision-making needs to extend beyond the short-term and consider long-term implications, much of what is at best murky at the time that decisions are made. Because they know they are working with imperfect information, they must acknowledge uncertainty and their fragility.

At the same time, they must take up accountability for the systems in which they function. They know the buck stops with them, even if almost everything in that system is outside of their control.

And leaders need to fully engage their whole selves to do these things and be this type of person. What constitutes and shapes the leader's self is therefore the topic of the next chapter.

Questions for reflection

Before proceeding to the next chapter, first take some time to reflect on these questions:

- What do I really value as a leader?
- What guides me in how I practice leadership on a daily basis?
- How much do I critically evaluate information?
- How open am I to imagine alternative ways to see situations?
- How can I help to create a more sustainable world?
- How can I integrate care, personal growth and accountability into my leadership journey?
- How do I intentionally build relationships as the core of leadership?
- Do I take personal responsibility for difficult decisions like layoffs?
- In what ways or areas can I lead more effectively?

Chapter 2

The leader's self

❖

I have used the phrase "our whole selves" several times in this book so far. What aspects of ourselves does this idea of the "whole self" refer to?

What constitutes a person and therefore a leader? What parts do we tend to neglect, or might we not even be aware of? What are those aspects of ourselves that we need to overcome the challenges we face?

When we ask ourselves questions such as who we are as leaders and how we should lead, we must first consider how we look at life and our place in it.

Worldviews

A worldview is precisely what the word implies – a way in which we view the world. We can think of it as a lens through which we look at life.

Our reality contains so much information that it is completely overwhelming to consider all of it as raw data all the time. This information overload is one of the reasons babies and toddlers sleep as much as they do. Making sense of their world is so overwhelming that they need more recovery time asleep than time awake. As adults, we also use sleep to process data.

As we grow older, we overcome this overwhelm by categorising, limiting and framing our reality in ways that make sense to us. One way we do so is through worldviews.

Worldviews provide ordering principles through which we view life. Our worldviews determine what we notice, how we think about those things and the environment we create for ourselves. A worldview also provides a framework that gives us "permission" to exclude other views.

Some types of worldviews are religious views and political frameworks, as well as different economic ideologies that define the role of individuals and society in terms of production, consumption and transfer of wealth.

Our worldviews influence how we think and act. As leaders, our worldviews therefore shape how we see or envision the future, as well as how we influence and create it for ourselves and others.

However, we do not always consider the fact that we do not fully see reality as it is. We are looking at it through the lens of our ideas, previous experiences and the things which have influenced us in life. As Anaïs Nin famously said: "We don't see things as they are, we see them as we are."

My career requires me to reflect daily on the challenges that leaders face and their lack of control over an exponential number of variables. This reflection continually reminds me of how limited our lens truly is.

Our worldviews, by definition, limit our perspective and can therefore create blind spots. As leaders, we must be especially careful of blindly believing the stories we tell ourselves and our own "headlines". We are complex beings who, by nature, are always aiming to protect our views. In the process, we can close ourselves to alternative perspectives.

One way of gaining clarity is regularly removing ourselves from the busyness and challenges of our day-to-day lives and spending time in solitude and reflection, as I expand on in more detail in later chapters.

I am not advocating that leaders should second guess every aspect of their reality every moment of the day. No person can function optimally in a constant state of re-evaluation. We will never be able to choose, commit and act that way. However, we can benefit from occasionally re-examining the lenses through which we view life, or at least becoming aware that they are there and that they do influence us.

Our worldviews are not static. Even though they were mostly formed without our conscious consent, we can consciously recreate them. Our actions are not only our response to how we have made sense of the world; they also shape how we perceive the world.

We can take actions that change our worldviews. For instance, we can read a book, listen to a podcast, or attend a seminar that argues for some points we do not agree with. By opening ourselves to the possible validity of those viewpoints, we can reassess our own.

Of course, the very point that we can consciously change our point of view is a point of view. In other words, that point of view is part of my worldview. I would argue that having a worldview that supports growth and allows one to be open to new views of reality is important for any leader. It is becoming ever more so because of our global reality discussed so far, which forces us to be much more agile in how and what we see.

It is also one of my concerns about AI. By design, it tracks our activities and suggests more of the same. This can cause people to get further entrenched in the status quo instead of questioning and challenging it to move forward.

The western worldview

Our worldviews are shaped by many personal aspects of our lives, like our childhood, early experiences, and the environment in which we grew up and matured, including our families, friends, schools and universities. These experiences would have been different for each of us.

However, as people living in the twenty-first century, many of our experiences were influenced by a particular set of philosophies and ideologies that dominated the past few decades. By philosophies and ideologies, I simply mean the ways large parts of humanity think about life and how they order their daily lives accordingly.

The way that most people think about leadership, business and organisations is heavily influenced by a set of ideas that is known as the western worldview. The roots of the western worldview can be traced back millennia to the teachings of the Greek philosophers, Plato and Aristotle. More recent philosophers and scientists who shaped the western worldview include Descartes and Isaac Newton.

I highlight a few of the key assumptions of the western worldview here so that you can become aware that this viewpoint shaped your perception of truth and reality.

- **Rationalism**

  The French philosopher Descartes defined human existence with the phrase, "I think therefore I am". This idea of a person as a thinking subject led to the theory of rationalism. Rationalism holds that the exercise of reason provides the only valid basis for action or belief. It also sees reason as the prime source of knowledge and spiritual truth.

- **Dualism**

  The idea of a person as a thinking subject led to many forms of dualism: body vs.. spirit, profane vs. sacred, and the world vs. the church, to name a few.

- **Individual autonomy**

  Individual autonomy is the belief in the primary importance of the individual and in the virtues of self-reliance and personal independence.

- **Materialism**

  According to materialism, the economic aspect of reality – money, profit, wealth and possessions – are viewed as absolute. Materialism sees the material reality – what we can experience with our senses, as more important than any spiritual reality.

- **Reductionism**

  Reductionist thinking is an attempt or tendency to explain complex phenomena or structures by relatively simple principles. According to reductionism, absolute knowledge, control and equilibrium are possible through reductionist thinking.

- **Mechanistic paradigm**

  The mechanistic paradigm approaches human systems, such as organisations, as if they are machines instead of living organisms.

As human beings, we find comfort in the safety of the familiar. People tend to identify with a label proudly. *I am a materialist. I am an individualist.*

While it is good to have clear views, we must remember that it is only a view. If we trace our worldviews back to their sources, only a very few thinkers in the history of human existence have shaped our ideas about life and our place in it. Most of us are not even aware of who those thinkers were who first conceived of the ideas about life and reality that we now hold and what motivated them to conceptualise life as they did.

Some of the paradigms mentioned above that underpin the western worldview have served us as humans, however, not all of them have, and none of these views fully capture the entire truth of our existence. They are just views and ideas.

In the past hundred-odd years, philosophy and science alike have questioned and disproven many of these paradigms. Despite this, these ways of thinking have remained with us. The western worldview is still the primary paradigm that defines the way we do business and lead our organisations, even though much of it is not working. As leaders, it is wise for us to remember that.

In recent years, I've seen leaders struggle to think beyond the assumptions of their western worldview when they need to think about China and its growing power, especially in Asia and Africa. For instance, there is clear evidence that China has a long-term strategy for getting involved in Africa. Because leaders with a western worldview tend to focus on shorter term outcomes than the Chinese worldview, it seems as if they are struggling to anticipate what this means for the sustainable growth of the organisations and even nations that they lead.

Questions to ask of your worldview

You might be reading this book and not identify very strongly with the western worldview, especially if you are younger or grew up in a non-western culture. However, that does not mean that your worldview is exempt from blind spots. All of us have a worldview, and therefore all of us can hold biases.

Until recently, many societies functioned as closed systems. For example, in countries where only one religion or political ideology is allowed by law, people tend to have the same culture and hold the same views about life.

However, globalisation, democratisation and technology, especially the internet and social networks, have opened up some of those closed systems. This openness is not necessarily supported by leaders who want to control people. However, whether they like it or not, people are becoming aware of alternative worldviews than the ones they were exposed to before.

This book is not about arguing the merits or not of particular ideologies or philosophies. I merely want to make you aware of the following:

- There are different points of view.

- Where and how we grow up can shape our worldview, often for life.

- Each point of view makes sense to the people who hold it.

- We all have certain points of view, whether we are aware of it or not.

- Our worldviews are often shaped by the ideas of only a very few influential thinkers.

- Our points of view shape how we view the world and, therefore, how we lead.

- We only know in part, and there is always more to discover and experiment with.

- Until recently, the world was a closed system, but global forces are opening it up more and more.

The tripartite self

Although it is based on my worldview, I want to offer you a way to think about yourself that I have found useful. It is a model that underpinned my study, and the findings of my research confirmed its usefulness.

You might find that you hold a similar view of yourself – or you may not. Either way, consider whether you find this model helpful or not. At a minimum, I would like to introduce this way of conceiving of the self because I will be using it in the chapters to follow.

The model is that of the tripartite self, in other words, that we consist of three parts: body, soul and spirit. These three parts are not distinct from each other but function together as an integrated whole.

Let's start with the most obvious part of ourselves: our body. It is that part of us that we can see and touch and that doctors and scientists can probe and dissect. Through the body's five senses, we interact with and are conscious of the world around us.[24]

Most of us will agree that there is more to us than our bodies. According to the model of the tripartite self, beyond our body we also have a soul, which refers to our thinking, will and emotions.

According to this model, the soul refers to more than our brainpower. The soul needs the brain, yes. Some researchers see the emergence of the soul at around 8-10 months of age, when children's reason, will and emotions start appearing.[25] However, we *are* not our brain. We *have* a brain, and we use it to think, feel and decide.[26]

The value of thinking and reason is self-evident to leaders. We analyse, strategise and synthesise. Our cognitive capacity is one of our key assets as leaders, even if we are not traditionally "intelligent" as defined or labelled by psychologists.

Leaders also intuitively know the importance of a strong will. We feel confident that we know what we need and want, and we are comfortable with advocating and even enforcing our will, not necessarily from a place of arrogance, but because we believe it is right.

Especially early in our leadership journey, we want to be independent and assert ourselves. I often see gifted young leaders build up a lot of 'evidence' that they are 'right'. These leaders are exceptional individual contributors who are in the top 5% of the population in terms of cognitive ability, yet they battle to understand that the other 95% of the population do not 'get it' as quickly, which can cause a lot of conflict with subordinates, peers and superiors.

As we mature as leaders, however, we tend to increasingly value others' contributions and collaboration. We learn to sometimes lose the battle of proving ourselves to be right to win the more important war of gaining a valuable ally. Instead of being independent, we become interdependent.

We also understand the power and therefore the importance of our emotions and those of others. It is important that we use our reason, but our emotions energise and propel us. For many of us as leaders, the emergence of the concept of emotional intelligence the last few years has simply confirmed what we intuitively knew. We must be aware of our own emotions to know how to work with people, and we must take others' emotions into account if we are going to be effective leaders.

However, a strong soul is not enough to guarantee success as a leader. I have seen and known leaders who are what I call "super souls". A super soul is a very intelligent person with exceptional aspects of emotional skills and business competencies who has been able to optimise the compounding effect of global business and political, religious and social systems for their personal gain. They are often much admired – until the bottom falls out and their selfish and unethical behaviours are exposed.

Two examples of people who could be described as super souls come to mind for me due to the destruction they left behind. One is the very successful American financier Jeffrey Epstein, who was convicted as a sex offender and subsequently was reported to have committed suicide in jail while awaiting trial. The other is the former CEO of Steinhoff, Marcus Jooste, under whose leadership certain accounting practices wiped out billions of dollars' worth of share value when those practices came to light.

Not all super souls are exposed. We follow them when they are successful, and they provide systemic benefits to many around them. The system maintains, supports and enhances certain of their behaviours. However, we all sense the difference between arrogant, self-made leaders and those who lead in service of others, even if it is only a vague feeling. I believe it is because there is more to leadership than the dimension of our souls. Thinking, will and emotions are not enough to make a truly great leader. It is why I find the tripartite model so useful.

Many people view the terms *soul* and *spirit* as synonymous. For example, some people speak about body, mind and soul, where *soul* refers to *spirit*.

However, I find the words *mind* and *soul* are too limited to describe our full selves. I find the tripartite model of the self that defines them as inherently different much more helpful. In addition to our soul, we have a spirit.

As I mentioned before, your spirit is your "inner source". While your soul is linked to your body in terms of brain development and capacity, your spirit transcends and exists beyond your body.

Spirituality is a personal and uniquely individualised construct. In the broadest possible sense, it involves beliefs, practices and experiences that provide people with direction, meaning, wholeness, guidance and connectedness.

People's spiritual experiences can be related to themselves, other people, nature, the universe, God or some other supernatural power. It often involves a desire to transcend or transform yourself, connect with a higher reality or being, and to be of service to others and the world. For some people, but not everyone, spirituality involves religion, in other words, a particular set of spiritual practices and beliefs.

I believe that our spirit also includes our conscience. To me, our consciences encompass much more than feeling guilty about something because of how we were raised, which will be different for each person. I can clearly distinguish when I'm being convicted of something in my spirit as opposed to feeling guilty because of how I was raised. I believe this type of spiritual conviction comes from God speaking to our spirit.

Every leader has their own construct of the spiritual, of course. Whatever yours is, I want to invite you to consider the perspective that there is an unknown realm beyond ourselves and that its existence prompts us to ask questions about the core of our existence. In the words of Albert Einstein: "What is incomprehensible is beyond the realm of science. It is in the realm of God."

Consider entertaining the thought that you could be open to an experience, a voice, a presence, a thought beyond your rational mind and the realm of the soul. In fact, like me, you might have already had such experiences and even hold them dear. If you are open to it, spirituality can guide your daily decision-making beyond the purely rational.

I consider the place that spirituality can have in leadership and our organisations more fully in Chapter 9. There, I discuss the role that spiritual awareness plays in leadership that produces sustainable results, as uncovered by my PhD research. Before we get there, however, we will first consider the first six dimensions, all of which form part of the dimension of our souls.

However, it might be useful to keep this idea of your spirit as something more than your soul in mind as you read the chapters that focus on the soul.

Alternative premises to consider

Based on the discussion of systems thinking, worldviews and who we are as people that have been covered so far, I want to offer you some alternative premises of life and leadership. In other words, these are ways to think about yourself as a leader and the world in which you lead that differs from conventional ways of thinking and doing.

1. The nature of reality is such that the world cannot be fully known, predicted and controlled, and that not all data are accessible to us.

2. Science provides a good foundation for the grounds of knowledge, but it is only a limited view. Knowledge can also be more subjective, spiritual or transcendental.

3. Humans have free will and can make free choices, but we are limited in our choices by our thinking and circumstances.

4. To change our viewpoints, we must understand why we think what we think.

5. A more subjective approach, which includes reflection, is required to consider the spiritual self of a leader.

6. Our construct of spirituality and whether we experience it or not is our choice.

These premises underpin and were confirmed by my research, which is why they form the foundation of the findings which I share with you in the chapters to follow. What makes sense to you and how you choose to apply these premises (or not), however, rests with you.

Questions for reflection

Before proceeding, I suggest that you reflect on the following questions:

• What do you perceive reality to be?

• What is a human being?

• What happens to a person at death?

• How is it possible to know things?

• How do we know what is right or wrong?

• What is the meaning of human history?

• What role does my body, soul and spirit each play in how I lead?

- What do I view my spirit to be? How open am I do consider a spiritual reality?

You might also find it helpful to consider how those you lead and work with would answer these questions, and how their answers might differ from yours.

SECTION 2

UNLEASHING THE LEADER'S FULL POTENTIAL

❖

This chapter and the ones that follow examine each of the seven dimensions which make up the leadership framework that emerged from my PhD study. In each chapter, I explain what that dimension entails and why it is important in leadership. I also offer practical ways to apply them.

Section 2 (Chapters 3 to 6) focuses on the four dimensions that make up the vertical oval of the framework. These dimensions all relate to leaders' drive to unleash their potential. They are mindfulness (Chapter 3), inspired creativity (Chapter 4), creating infinite possibilities (Chapter 5) and clarity of direction (Chapter 6).

Section 3 (Chapters 7 and 8) focus on the horizontal oval of the framework, which relates to leaders' drive to connect with others through relationships. Chapter 7 covers unconditional engagement and Chapter 8 humane connectivity.

These first six dimensions mostly relate to a leader's soul, in other words, their thinking, will and emotions. Section 4 (Chapter 9) discusses the seventh dimension, spiritual awareness, which focuses on the leader's spirit.

Keep in mind as you read these chapters that the dimensions do not function in isolation. Not only do they influence each other, but many leadership practices touch on more than one dimension. The dimensions seek to paint a picture of integrated leadership instead of disparate practices.

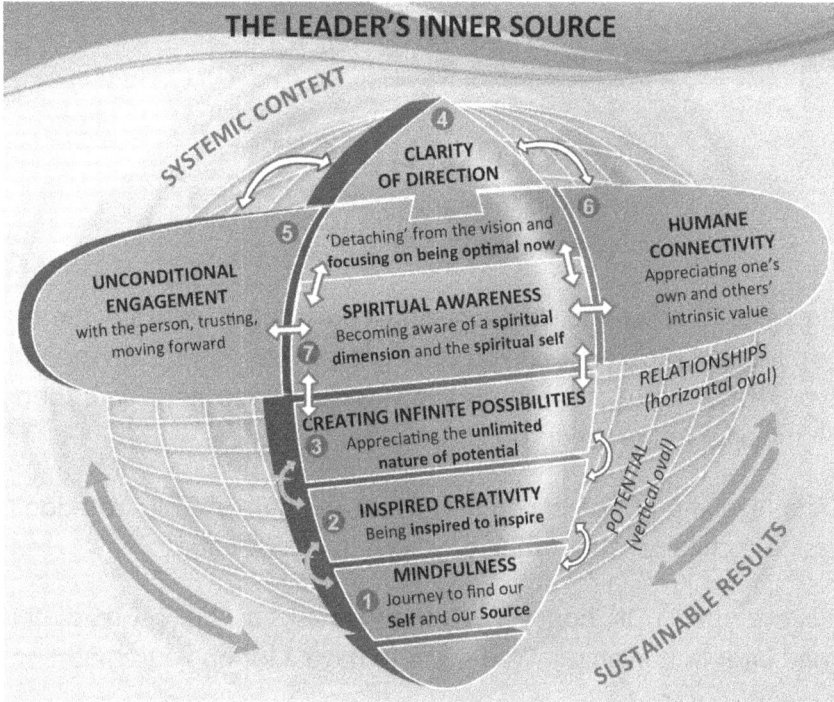

THE LEADER'S INNER SOURCE

SYSTEMIC CONTEXT

4 CLARITY OF DIRECTION

5 'Detaching' from the vision and focusing on being optimal now

6 HUMANE CONNECTIVITY
Appreciating one's own and others' intrinsic value

UNCONDITIONAL ENGAGEMENT
with the person, trusting, moving forward

SPIRITUAL AWARENESS
Becoming aware of a spiritual dimension and the spiritual self

7 CREATING INFINITE POSSIBILITIES
3 Appreciating the unlimited nature of potential

RELATIONSHIPS
(horizontal oval)

INSPIRED CREATIVITY
2 Being inspired to inspire

POTENTIAL
(vertical oval)

MINDFULNESS
1 Journey to find our Self and our Source

SUSTAINABLE RESULTS

Chapter 3

Mindfulness

❖

Imagine this scenario. You're having a busy day at work and there's a particular problem that you can't get off your mind. Even though you're in and out of meetings and video calls, you don't contribute optimally. You're preoccupied.

That evening at home, you're quiet at the dinner table. You don't ask the children about their day like you usually do.

"Is everything OK, honey?" your spouse asks as you get ready for bed later that evening. "You seem to have a lot on your mind."

"Just mulling over something from work," you answer.

Without having to say so, both of you know you will be tossing, turning and fretting about this problem all night. And you'll probably wake up with a blistering headache even though you must face another busy day.

Leadership means facing problems that don't have easy solutions. Unfortunately, worrying about them has become a norm for many leaders. The problem arises when worry becomes a consuming downward spiral with a negative effect on your productivity, decisions and relationships.

So what do the most successful leaders do to counter these natural tendencies to worry and stress? A practice called *mindfulness*, the first of the seven leadership dimensions.

THE LEADER'S INNER SOURCE

SYSTEMIC CONTEXT

MINDFULNESS
Journey to find our
Self and our **Source**

SUSTAINABLE RESULTS

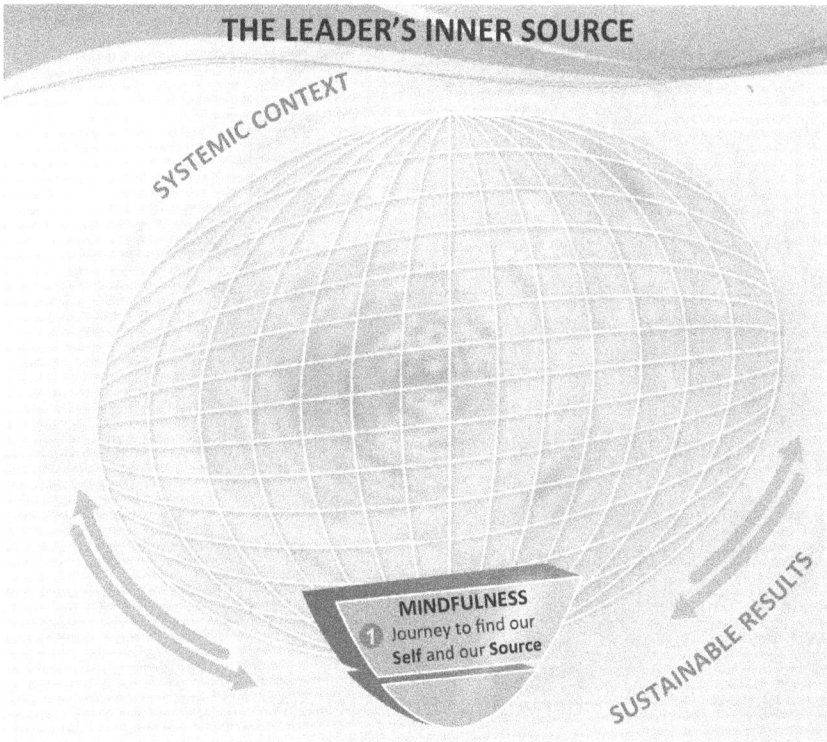

What is mindfulness?

Even though the term *mindfulness* is growing in popularity, many people only have a vague idea of what it refers to. In some circles, it is used as an important spiritual practice. For our purposes, mindfulness is the ability to be present, to be attuned to our surroundings, to be aware of what we are thinking, feeling and sensing, and to live moment by moment. It is about paying attention to what is happening now or, in other words, what we are paying attention to.

Mindfulness is all about awareness, especially self-awareness relative to our systemic context. If we think of ourselves as body, soul and spirit, it means that we can grow in awareness of all these aspects of our selves.

What are we thinking and feeling? What impact do our thoughts and emotions have on our bodies, and what effect does the state of our bodies have on our thoughts and feelings? Mindfulness also extends to the spirit – becoming aware of when and how we tap into our inner source or a higher Source.

A tangible place to start with mindfulness is with our bodies. Because of the western worldview's emphasis on the materialistic and tangible, it emphasises the body over the spirit and the soul, as is evident in the advertising media. Even though we are more than our bodies, we can use awareness of our bodies to grow our awareness of our souls and spirits.

For example, we can use breathing exercises to focus on our breathing patterns. Being aware of the feeling of air coming in and out of our bodies relieves stress and allows us to get connected with our bodies.

However, on the other side of the spectrum, we can also become so fixated with our bodies that it limits our awareness beyond the physical self.

As our sense of awareness grows, so does our sense of connection with ourselves. We can function as an integrated whole. This sense of awareness and connection can extend beyond ourselves to others and the world around us. It can even include a connection with a reality beyond the physical world, as we will explore in more depth in Chapter 9 when we consider the importance of spiritual awareness and ourselves in a cosmic context.

Our sense of awareness and connection can also grow from the inside out. As we become more aware and connected to our thoughts and feelings, we become more mindful of our bodies. The same is true for spiritual awareness. As we gain spiritual awareness and connection, we become more mindful of our bodies and souls.

The importance of mindfulness

We are all on the journey of life, and we are each finding our way forward. Across many ways of thinking about life and our place in it, the essence of our journey is conceptualised to be about finding ourselves and living a grounded life, connecting with and living in connection to our source, and contributing to others and a cause bigger than ourselves.

Mindfulness is important because it helps us find our best way forward in the dynamic, complex, cosmic system which is our life journey. Mindfulness helps us become aware of the potential available to us. Some of that potential is inside us, like our brainpower, willpower and emotions. Other sources of potential are outside of us, like relationships, nature and a Higher Power. Through being present with high levels of self-awareness, we can access these internal and external sources.

Unfortunately, we often complicate our journeys for ourselves by carrying "baggage" with us. This baggage makes the journey unnecessarily hard for us and others. Mindfulness helps us get rid of our baggage piece by piece and situation by situation.

Getting rid of our baggage is not easy, but it is very important, especially for us as leaders. Leaders are accountable – the buck usually stops with us – but often we look for the solution to a problem outside of ourselves first. In a conflict situation, for example, we see the mistake the other person made first. It is human nature to do so. It is much harder to see our part in the problem first.

If I walk into a store to receive a service, I might encounter a service person who is not able to deliver that service, or at least not in the way that I expected. I get irritated at this person who is incapable of doing their job and at this company that does not see the importance of customer service.

Even though those points might be valid, they are not the most productive place to start. I must first take up responsibility for my part in the situation before I can effectively address the rest. Perhaps I was not courteous enough, or I did not explain what I wanted clearly enough. Perhaps I was speaking to the wrong person; I expected a service that the person in front of me was simply not trained to provide. Expectations that are not clarified can be the cause of many challenges in our own mind first.

One of my mentors, the late Dr David Hendry, suggested that executives ask themselves this question: *What is it about me relative to this person or situation that I am uncomfortable with?* The emphasis here is on the phrase *about me*.

In my previous example, I might own that I had walked into the store in an irritable mood, and my mood, influenced my ability to explain my need clearly. Once I am more aware of my own emotions and deal with them first, I am in a far better position to deal with the situation, and especially the other people involved, more constructively.

As we get ourselves out of the way, we can deal more effectively with others.

Mindfulness for leaders

Every person can benefit from mindfulness because it allows us to engage our whole selves in any situation in life, however it is especially important for leaders.

To continue the journey metaphor, leaders are on an expedition in a world characterised by a web of known and unknown relationships. They not only have to find their own clarity and way forward, but must also provide clarity for and lead others.

Leaders must take the disparate journeys of everyone they are leading into account to forge a collective journey for the organisation or group they are leading. They are always challenged by confusion, seeking, striving and a requirement to provide clarity. Through this all, leaders must have and give clear direction and see a future vision towards which to guide others.

Well-developed or so-called "natural" leaders often possess immense brainpower, a powerful will and strong emotional potential which enable them to forge ahead. However, without a sense of higher purpose, such leaders can often end up as "super souls" – great leaders who have not achieved what they are capable of or of sustainable value for all their effort and giftedness.

In the ultimate journey of life, these super souls might even be considered to have failed. They are not living grounded lives true to themselves, they have no or little connection with their Source, and they have only lived in service of their selfish ideals. And while it's easy to think of these people as "they", in reflecting on my own leadership journey and that of others, I'm continually reminded that we are all fallible.

Leadership can be so much more. True leadership which leads to sustainable results employs the talents and skills of the leader in service of creating a context where others can excel and become the best that they are meant to be. Through mindfulness, these leaders get themselves and their baggage out of the way and create a space where others can grow and contribute to the greater vision.

Mindfulness is an approach that allows leaders to go beyond the limitations of their egos in their daily lives, care for others and have constructive relationships. Mindfulness helps leaders pay attention to all that is happening in and around them and sense their inner source. If a person so wishes, mindfulness can open the door for leaders to become aware of and tap into a Higher Source during every act of leadership.

A few years ago, an exceptionally gifted leader told me that he could not afford *not* to be 100% present at all times. If he is not present in every moment, he feels that he might miss a piece of the puzzle that could give him access to the next big deal. For that reason, he avoids anything that could get him in a position where he would lose focus even for a few minutes, for example, excessive alcohol consumption.

Being present in the moment is an invaluable habit that any leader is wise to cultivate.

How to practice mindfulness

Practicing mindfulness is not about aspiring to some ideal state. It's about creating and building upon habits that keep you in a state of mindfulness more often.

Mindfulness can be practiced in many ways. Prayer and meditation are popular methods, but it can also be as simple as taking a few moments to quiet your mind and body. For example, go for a walk, read a chapter of a book or take a moment to sit quietly.

Many of my coaching clients have found that coaching helps them practice mindfulness. The coach as a sounding board can assist us in becoming aware of what we are saying which follows what we think. Because great coaches make effective use of questioning, they can assist us to become more mindful.

As you start experiencing the benefits of mindfulness, build from there.

As a leader, I believe you can and should benefit from practicing mindfulness in times of solitude, however you'll want to grow to a place where you can practice mindfulness in any situation.

For instance, when you're in an important meeting or having a difficult conversation, pay attention to what you are thinking, feeling and sensing.

You might be surprised that you catch yourself displaying an egotistical attitude that has a negative impact on yourself or others. Or you might become aware of some greed that points to an unhealthy preoccupation with yourself and your own short-term needs.

I aim to approach my coaching conversations with clients in a mindful manner. A client recently asked me after eight years of coaching, "How do we take the coaching to the next level?" I thought about it for a few days, and then I realised that I need to start by taking my level of preparation and mindfulness to the next level.

When I focus on being mindful, I am often surprised at the prompts that come to me. For instance, while facilitating an onsite session, a tragic accident occurred that caused the death of two employees. During the week that followed, at one point I felt prompted to get up and hug the leader in whose area the accident had happened. The hug lasted a few seconds longer than either of us expected, and in these moments, I was intensely aware of the pain of the leader. To me, it was beyond an experience of deep emotions, will or the mind – it was a spiritual experience.

When I coach leaders in very complex situations, I listen very carefully and ask well thought through questions. However, I also often ask for internal guidance on what to ask next and how. As a coach, the right question at the right time is critical, and we can easily miss it if we do not pay careful attention.

A few years ago, I coached a COO who said to me, "I am an introvert, and I cannot represent the company out there". I challenged him to think of this belief as a label that he had accepted and which almost always goes along with not taking up the challenge (or the responsibility) to grow and put ourselves out there with confidence.

At the end of six months of coaching, he mentioned to me that that challenge I had given him at the start of the coaching process made a big difference in how he led. He was able to represent the company with more confidence and was able to grow in new ways.

For us as coaches and psychologists, identifying and challenging limiting beliefs like this require that we must be 100% present in the moment.

For any other leader, consistently operating in mindfulness sets the stage for the rest of the leadership dimensions to come into full force.

Mindfulness in action

Let's return to the scenario of the preoccupied leader at the start of this chapter and reimagine what it would be like if you would incorporate some mindfulness practices.

You're having a busy day at work, and there's a particular problem that you can't get off your mind.

On the way home in the car, you slowly breathe in and out a few times to give yourself time to get perspective on your day, just as you and your coach discussed you'd do. As you do so, you realise that you were preoccupied with this one problem and not fully present, even during meetings.

You also realise that your assistant looked a bit despondent, and you remember that she was taking her son to see a therapist this week. You didn't even notice it to ask how things are going.

You make a mental reminder to ask her how it's going first thing tomorrow, and you decide to be intentional about being more present with your family when you get home.

You're a bit quieter during dinner, but you laugh at the kids' stories and make sure to give them each a hug before bed.

"You were quieter than usual this evening," your spouse mentions when you get ready for bed. "Is there something on your mind?"

"Yes, a tough situation at work," you say and proceed to explain the situation at a high level. Your spouse is great at lending a sympathetic ear, and you often get good insights from explaining things to someone who's not as intimately involved in the situation.

Before you switch the light off to go to sleep, you pray and have quiet time as usual.

You wake up refreshed the next morning and go for your usual cycle. In the shower afterwards, you suddenly get an idea. You excitedly dress and get in the car where you think through your brainwave in more detail.

As you walk into the office, your assistant is already there. You're excited to share your idea, but you check yourself. Instead, you first ask how the appointment went. She's grateful that you remembered, and she mentions that you seem to be in a different mood than the day before. You proceed to tell her about your idea, and you two brainstorm next steps.

Is it always as simple as that? Certainly not.

But whether it's having a regular time to reflect, talking to your spouse, spending time in prayer, or riding your bike in the fresh morning air, we can create opportunities to pause and become more mindful.

Questions for reflection

Before you proceed to the next chapter, reflect on these questions:

- Do I have daily practice (prayer, meditation, recording daily priorities, exercise, time in nature, etc.) that enables me to let go of the noise of the past and go into each day with clarity? How consistently do I practice it?

- How willing am I to tap into a higher Source beyond my own soul or a source outside myself for guidance?

- How intentional am I about being 100% present wherever I am? How consistently do I practice it?

- How consistently do I consider what others need as I go through the day?

- How aware am I of my surroundings and the bigger systemic context?

Chapter 4

Inspired creativity

❖

I often marvel at how some people can see and create things long before others. They display a level of creativity that seems inspired – the second leadership dimension.

We all know about the creative minds of our times like Steve Jobs and Elon Musk, but every industry and niche has their own people like that.

For example, one of the people in the field of my industry, executive coaching and organisational psychology, that comes to mind is Prof Dough Waldo, the author and developer of the REACH profile. He is a truly an inspired person, researcher and developer who saw further what most of us could to develop new angles to the way we think about leadership.

I'm generally very cautious about the use of assessments and profiles. If they are used without discretion and a deeper understanding of the person and their systemic context, profiles and assessments can become a limiting label. Think back, for example, to the introverted COO I mentioned in the previous chapter.

However, when the feedback on assessments and profiles are facilitated well, they can awaken new thoughts and open new paths for people and organisations. After personally completing the 360 REACH profile about eight years ago, I became much more aware of how to handle situations that involve difficult power dynamics in organisations. The profile's feedback made me aware of alternative approaches.

I've now used the REACH profile in my coaching practice for over a thousand profiles and numerous team interventions. During that time, I have seen how the feedback resulting from the REACH profile can inspire individuals and teams to think about their approach to leadership in new ways.

That is the wonderful thing about an inspired tool like the REACH profile: it is also a source of inspiration for others.

Exactly how it plays out might differ from industry to industry and case to case, but the same principles apply. Let's take a look at what they are.

Inspired creativity

Inspired creativity is about finding alternative solutions and approaches to obtain sustainable results.

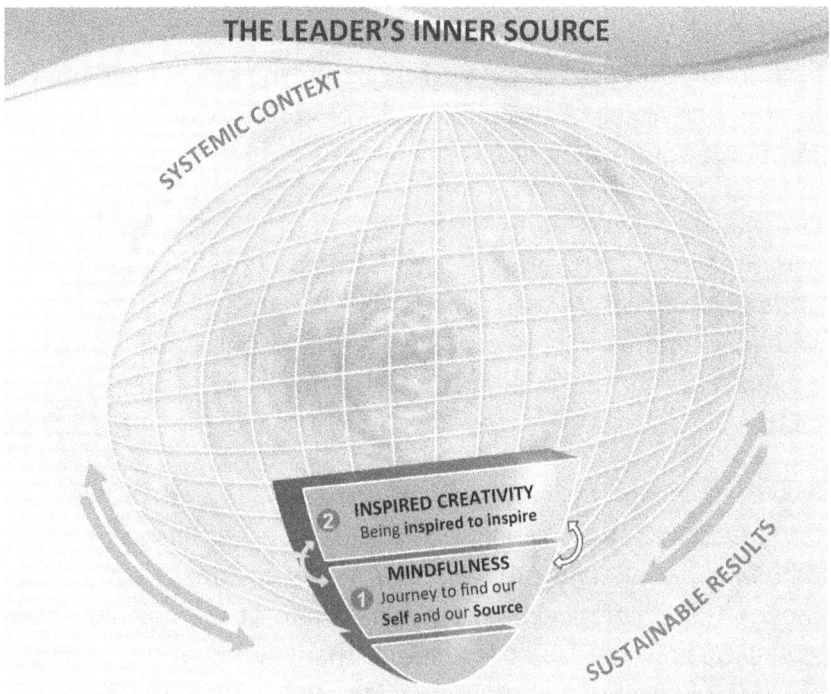

THE LEADER'S INNER SOURCE

SYSTEMIC CONTEXT

INSPIRED CREATIVITY
Being inspired to inspire

MINDFULNESS
Journey to find our
Self and our Source

SUSTAINABLE RESULTS

The chaotic and volatile global system in which we function requires us to seek solutions that go beyond the obvious. As leaders, we need to take a broader and longer-term view of the challenges we face.

To see possibilities and potential outcomes that extend beyond our current reality, we must be able to recognise patterns, integrate seemingly unrelated events, suspend what we know, accept that some things are unknowable and be open to different views. As much as possible, we must also be aware of the systemic impact of our decisions.

After grounding our thinking in data, such foresight is driven by creative thinking much more than analytical reasoning. It is about creating a future state and not focusing on understanding the past only. It requires a shift in perception, orientation, thinking and values.

While the challenges of our time are changing very rapidly, most leaders' ability and capacity to cope with these challenges have not grown at the same speed. One reason is our limited view of what we are capable of. We cannot rely only on our reason. We also need to tap into our intuition – our mind's ability to connect and integrate diverse stimuli and insights coming from inside and outside ourselves. Our complex, volatile and uncertain world requires leaders to tap into their creativity as well as that of others to reach the future they envision.

Much has been written about the importance of experimentation and innovation in organisations and especially in business. I agree with it wholeheartedly. However, creativity underpins experimentation and innovation. The leader's role, therefore, is to create an environment where creativity is possible and can flourish.

To do that, my research uncovered that a leader has two responsibilities: be inspired, firstly, and then inspire others.

Be inspired

Leadership and high-stress situations are almost synonymous. Unfortunately, our brains' natural response to stress is the opposite of what is needed to be creative.

When we stress, our brains produce fast beta brainwaves that help us focus on the task at hand. However, they make us less creative and less emotionally aware. There is nothing wrong with beta brainwaves, but this state of being has its limitations. Moreover, being stuck in beta mode leads to anxiety and burn out, a very real challenge for many leaders.

When we are faced with problems and challenges that we cannot solve with analytical thinking, producing beta brainwaves is counterproductive. We need to be creative, not overly analytical. Creativity happens when our brainwaves slow down to alpha frequency. During alpha, we are calm and present in the moment. We are open to see new possibilities and make new connections. We are also much more attuned to the emotional states of others, allowing us to draw on the strengths of our team and network.

Operating in alpha when we are faced with complex challenges and problems is not natural. It is a skill and habit we must grow. However, it is available to us as per our design. Just because we are not utilising what we are capable of does not mean that it is not there. Science is continually uncovering new aspects of how our brains and bodies functions that show us that there is more available to us than what most of us are aware of. We just need to learn to access it.

Spending regular time in solitude, prayer, reflection and meditation, for example, slows down our brainwaves. When our brainwaves slow down from beta to alpha, we get rid of the noise in our head. In this state of calm, we can gain clarity on our next step. We give ourselves a psychologically safe space in which to operate – which is the first step to be able to create that space for others too.

Having a clear source of inspiration also helps us to access, nurture and revitalise our creativity consciously. The leaders I have worked with who have clarity on their sources of inspiration are calmer and more present. Even in high-stress situations, they can think clearly and come up with creative ideas without effort.

Many people, including myself and Prof Dough Waldo of the REACH profile, find inspiration in their spiritual Source, such as God. Many religions hold that humans are created beings and that we derive our creativity from the Creative Source that created us. People also get inspired by nature, art, people, certain relationships in their lives as well as acts of kindness, whether it is their own or others'.

While it's good to know the tried and tested practices that inspire us, we should also change things up and explore something new every so often. It's why experiences like holidays, travel and conferences often spark new ideas or inspire fresh motivation. Discovering something new about yourself can do the same.

Take note that there's a difference between motivation and inspiration. Leaders are almost always motivated people. However, the sources of their motivation are not always inspirational. Many sources of motivation, such as immediate gratification, short-term wealth, fear or pride, most often do not lead to sustainable results for yourself or others.

While such sources of motivation can result in creativity, too, it is not the kind that produces the sustainable results we are talking about in this book. To get those types of results, leaders need more than motivation. They need inspiration.

Inspire others

Many popular movies feed on the idea of a lone, heroic leader. Despite their flaws, this person single-handedly swoops in to save the day.

Unfortunately, it very seldom, if ever, works like that in the real world. While our need for a hero causes us to give credit to the leader when things go well or blame the leader when it does not, the reality is that leaders always operate in a leadership system which relies on a web of relationships.

Leaders themselves also mistakenly try to live up to this unrealistic ideal of the lone, heroic leader. They gather all the problems that fall under their leadership onto their own shoulders (or desks). They then gather a select few like-minded individuals behind closed doors to come up with the solutions to fix it all.

In reality, leaders often only have a very limited grasp of the full extent of the problems at hand. Especially when a radical shift in thinking and behaviours is required, it is essential to involve others with different views. There is wisdom in the collective. No single person can know it all or know enough to figure out complex, systemic problems alone.

To solve the complex problems of our current reality, leaders must enable those they lead to be creative problem solvers too. As much as a leader needs to be inspired, those they lead need to be inspired as well. Diversity of opinions and views can yield amazingly creative solutions to problems.

Being inspired ultimately always remains the responsibility of an individual. It is every person's choice whether and to what extent they will be inspired.

However, a leader has the responsibility to create an environment where inspiration and thus creativity can flow easily and naturally. Sadly, they can also make it almost impossible for any inspiration or creativity to surface. The leader determines the level of inspiration and creativity that is possible under their leadership.

This is the reason why I often say to leaders to focus on their own development 90% of the time, and others will get the benefit of who they are as an inspired leader.

Inspiration in conversation

Much like the image of the lone hero, inspiration is also often depicted as a mystical experience that you have all by yourself. And it certainly can happen that way.

However, in practice, inspiration just as often or more occurs between people, especially when you encounter new ideas in conversation.

For example, when I conduct an assessment like the REACH profile, I insist on providing feedback in person. Yes, this is to keep the person from interpreting their results incorrectly. More importantly, though, it's because the principles are awakened most powerfully when people discuss the results.

I can often see how the different puzzle pieces start coming together in this conversation. People will usually reach a point where they say: this like, "This really makes sense now." Or they will say, "I didn't know my preferences are that extreme. I need to think and do more analysis before acting. I need to be softer on people as I push for results".

Their words often confirm that the breakthrough for them happened in conversation. For example, they will say, "Thank you for this conversation. It gives me more clarity on how I can approach leadership in a more inspired way and what I need to do to be more effective". Or something like, "This was meaningful and exciting. I'm amazed at how you were able to gather all this information from these questions".

People leave these conversations with more clarity and inspiration to grow.

I also facilitate assessments and conversations like these in a team context. Very recently, these conversations during a team alignment and strategy session made them aware how task-driven the team was that they lacked a focus on people. Only a few months later, more than one person in this team mentioned to me that they noticed a marked shift towards being more people-orientated.

It was in conversation that this team was inspired to make a cultural change that typically doesn't happen very easily.

How to inspire others

While it's wonderful when a group is inspired and aligned, that's not always the case. Especially if you're the leader who wants to inspire the people you lead.

So how do you inspire others?

I must emphasise that it starts with being inspired.

It's a natural progression. Being inspired leads to purpose and passion which, in turn, very naturally flows to the people around you. If those feelings are real, your words and actions will reflect them. The leader's only responsibility is to channel that purpose and passion into a clearly articulated vision and to live true to the values which underpin it.

Here are a few more points of action.

- **Reframe it**

    If you or those you lead come against challenges in pursuit of a vision, the first thing to do is to reframe the challenge as stimulating rather than threatening, as an opportunity instead of a risk.

    A threatening challenge immediately results in beta brainwaves, which inhibits creativity. When we are in a safe state, our blood readily transports oxygen to our brain, and we can think clearly. However, when we feel threatened, blood moves to the big organs for a flight-or-fight response, and the blood levels in the thinking part of our brain drop. That is why they say stress makes us stupid.

- **Replace negative patterns**

The irony is that our perception of threats is not always real – It is based on how we think because of our past. Unfortunately, the psychological views of people like Freud, Jung and others overemphasised healing the past, which has given the past too much power over us. We need to deal with the past and move on.

Letting go of the past is often one of the keys for leaders to move to the next level. We run the risk of gathering many rocks in our rucksack as we take some blows on our journey through life. We can replace these negative patterns by intentionally focusing on going forward. We're meant to look forward; our eyes are in the front of our heads, after all.

We often use the past as an excuse not to take responsibility for the challenges we face now. I often hear clients who are not functioning optimally say: "Something is holding me back. I am not sure why, and I am trying to understand what is causing the problem." However, we do not have to understand the past. We only need to recognise the thinking pattern that is not serving us, let go of it, and replace it with one that does.

I often work with executives who are able to engage much more effectively after realising that the way they see themselves, approach others and achieve results was held back by the baggage of the past. After working through it or intentionally deciding to let go of it they see a different future.

- **Find new ways**

Because of our brainwaves and our blood levels, people naturally go into survival mode in a threatening situation. They take a very limited approach by simply trying to recreate the previous status quo.

However, in a complex and ever-changing system, the previous status quo should be questioned. The status quo either no longer works, or it is not optimal anymore, hence the challenge.

Not only leaders but everyone around them must find a new way of doing things. While the leader can give direction on a high level, each person in that system will need to take responsibility and be creative to find their own new way too.

Sibu, the group CEO that I introduced at the beginning of this book, is excellent at involving others to find new ways. In strategic planning, he leads the way, but his executive team is as committed as he is to find creative solutions for very complex challenges.

- **See stimulating challenges**

This point follows closely on the previous one. As leaders, we can reframe that same situation as stimulating rather than threatening.

That does not mean we should sugar coat or downplay the real negative effects of a situation. For example, South Africa's national crisis of load shedding is causing widespread damage and suffering, even death.

However, instead of becoming overwhelmed, you can choose to challenge yourself to focus on what the challenge is that you can help solve. Instead of being a victim, you – and the people you lead – are now actors.

Every challenge is an opportunity to grow, learn and improve. Such a stimulating challenge produces excitement and curiosity; it invites experimentation and exploration.

Such a psychologically safe environment is what you as the leader, as well as those you lead, need to be creative. We use our design more optimally to come up with creative solutions. The ultimate result of the challenge is a better future and more sustainable results.

- **Offer a helping hand**

  In a psychologically safe environment, helping each other is obvious and inherently rewarding. Like the different parts of a body, different people in a system benefit themselves by helping others. If others are better off, so are you.

  This way of thinking and doing is not always common practice. Even in an organisation, people quickly see another person or department as competition or "the enemy". As the leader, model helping others for its own sake. Such generosity fuels creativity.

- **Use your words wisely**

  Inspiring others can also be as simple as sharing positive stories. Words are powerful tools that we use to create our reality and that of others. Leaders have a huge responsibility to choose their words very carefully and they should always aim to inspire.

  The words we use as leaders are especially so because they shape the thinking and actions of the people we lead. Our words set the emotional tone in our organisations, and they paint a picture of the potential future, or the vision, everyone in the organisation should be striving for.

  The leader's words paint a picture of the path ahead. We can paint a dark, threatening, unsafe picture, or we can invite people to be part of a stimulating, rewarding, inspiring, exciting and meaningful adventure. This is not always easy, for example in a process of restructuring where leaders have to create safety when they do not always feel safe.

The result

The type of leadership I am describing here involves less effort from the leader alone and relies more on their capacity to influence others positively and constructively.

I see it as a more spiritual approach to leadership. You are leading from the inside and the inspiration of your Source. In the process, you also allow each person you lead to live and work in a more inspired and authentic way that is true to themselves, their design and their Source.

You are creating an environment where everyone can engage more fully with themselves, those around them, and their world. They can then use this energy to obtain results for the good of the whole.

A leadership style of inspired creativity is not necessarily common. However, I see inspiring others not only as one of the keys to obtaining sustainable results as a leader but also as a powerful way to maintain trust and engagement.

If we are humble and authentic, if we take responsibility, hold others accountable and are ethical, we cement our credibility. People start to trust us and our leadership. They are inspired to believe in the future we envision and to be part of creating the exciting future that we are able to paint with them.

Questions for reflection

Before you proceed, take some time to reflect on these questions.

- Where do I find inspiration?
- Do I inspire others by being open to the limitless nature of creativity? Or do I dampen the creativity of others?
- Do I always see potential and steer away from labels?
- How much do I prioritise conversations that inspire me and others?
- How effective am I at creating a space where others feel safe enough to be creative?

Chapter 5

Creating infinite possibilities

❖

The next leadership dimension, creating infinite possibilities, flows naturally from inspired creativity. Inspiration and creativity allow you to become aware of more possibilities.

Once we get started, we realise that such possibilities are endless. The unlimited nature of potential opens up a whole new world. The future is not limited by potential but only by our inability to envision it.

If we can dare to allow this potential to unfold and not resist it, we can see tremendous growth. As Wheatley puts it:[27]

> *Uniqueness, free will and creativity pose enormous problems... Creativity is unwanted, because it is always surprising and is therefore uncontrollable [...] But all of life resists control. All of life reacts to any process that inhibits its freedom to create itself [...] Life is in motion, constantly creating, exploring, discovering. Nothing alive, including us, resists these great creative motions.*

Pratibha with her drive to make a positive impact and end world hunger, which I told you about at the start of the book, is an example of a leader who never ceases to create infinite possibilities. Nothing is impossible for Prathiba. She is highly ambitious, but she is also surprisingly patient in allowing possibilities to unfold that will bring her closer to achieving her aims.

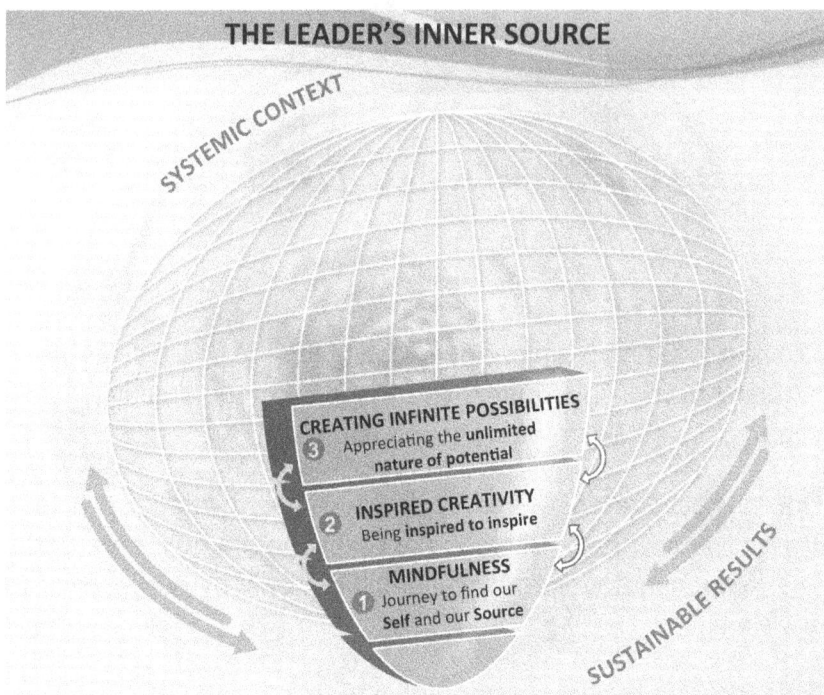

THE LEADER'S INNER SOURCE

SYSTEMIC CONTEXT

CREATING INFINITE POSSIBILITIES
③ Appreciating the unlimited nature of potential

INSPIRED CREATIVITY
② Being inspired to inspire

MINDFULNESS
① Journey to find our Self and our Source

SUSTAINABLE RESULTS

No defeat is final – it is only a hurdle that she will eventually overcome. And success does not stop her either, as it does for many people. When she conquered the corporate ladder, she went on to run her own company. And now she is stretching her wings beyond business leadership to influence global policy.

Let's take a closer look at how creating infinite possibilities work.

Infinite possibilities

The possibilities in our world are infinite because of the complex system in which we operate. Each of the billions of people in the world has a certain amount of agency – in other words, they can choose to think, feel and act in different ways in any given moment. Yes, those options are influenced by the systems in which they function, however each person has a free will; they have a choice.

All these people exercising their free will every moment – especially global leaders who are driving their own agendas – make our world unpredictable and chaotic. We do not know what will happen in the next hour, let alone further into the future. There are too many variables to consider. The possible permutations in our system of visible and invisible relationships are endless. And our world is becoming *more* unpredictable, not less.

One response to all this uncertainty is risk management. Assessing risks and planning for different scenarios based on their likelihood is essential. However, risk management and planning can only get us that far. It is a defensive strategy, not always a creative one. We have access to a richness of systemic resources that cannot be limited by predicting future results.

To obtain sustainable results and create a better future, leaders must become aware of, appreciate and embrace the unlimited nature of potential. Instead of seeing it as a risk or a threat, infinite possibilities contain tremendous creative potential. The present does not dictate the future; it is merely the starting point for an infinite number of paths into the future. Any creative future is possible if people dare to create it.

The unlimited potential of people

As leaders, we not only need to be aware of the infinite possibilities that lie in the future. We also need to be aware of the unlimited potential of people – ourselves, those we lead, those we serve and those who lie far beyond our sphere of influence. The unlimited potential of people makes it possible to realise the infinite possibilities which we envision.

That is why it is so important that leaders believe in people and develop them. The more the people around us become aware of their unlimited potential, that of others and the unlimited possibilities which exist as a result, the more likely we are to achieve our vision.

As with inspiration and creativity, it remains an individual's choice whether they are going to take hold of this view of themselves and the world. We as leaders can limit the possibilities for that person. In the context of the system where we are the leader, we set the ceiling of possibility. If we set the bar low, those we lead will either shrink back or move out from underneath our leadership to somewhere where their potential can be realised.

However, we can also do the opposite. We can create a context where people are reminded of their value and their potential. As leaders, we can often see the potential in others with more clarity than they can. By believing in people and developing them, we can open up possibilities for others so that their potential can be unleashed more fully.

While facilitating leadership development interventions that focus on creating a culture of coaching, my team and I often ask leaders about who has had the greatest impact on their career. The answer is almost always something like "those leaders in my life that believed in my potential even before I could see it". These influential leaders demonstrated that they believed in that person by giving them opportunities, valuing their opinion and pushing them forward.

The power of partnership

By ourselves, we are unlikely to change the status quo, but working with others opens up infinite possibilities. I was recently reminded of this truth when I entered into a new partnership.

I believe partnering with the right people in a mutually beneficial way creates more possibilities and allows us to realise more of them for the good of all. For instance, in my partnerships, I add value to their team and the clients we serve. In turn, the partnership gives me much more than extra work. I learn, grow and develop because of the relationships and methodologies I get exposed to.

While I believe in the power of partnerships, I believe we should enter into them with careful consideration. I only partner with organisations that view the leaders' primary role the same way I do: as raising the ceiling for those we lead so that we can co-create infinite possibilities with them.

With my most recent partnership, for example, I already became aware of the foundation of their work in the 1980s. At the time, they conducted research in the mining sector in South Africa, where I worked. Some of their findings struck a chord with me back then, so it is not surprising that their model, based on that original research, still resonates with me.

When our paths crossed again recently, I first attended some of their workshops to make sure that we were still aligned on our core values. I also had conversations with members of their team. We only formalised the partnership when both parties were convinced that we were a good fit for each other and the clients we'll serve together.

I realise that formal partnership as it applies to my business might not work for yours. However, the principle of partnership can also apply to your peers, other business units, or to the people you lead. It's about combining forces to create more and better outcomes than you would have on your own.

I encourage you: seek out opportunities where you can work with the right people. Evaluate each carefully, but do not hesitate to embrace it when you are well aligned. You can always let go when it's the end of a season.

Inhibiting thinking and behaviour

To unleash our unlimited potential as well as that of others, we must guard against inhibiting thinking, mindsets and behaviour.

In our attempt to understand ourselves, others and our world, we tend to want to control the unlimited nature of potential through the use of labels. Think back to the COO who capped his own career growth and impact because of labelling himself as an introvert.

When something is labelled, by definition, we limit it. If we can put it in a box, we feel that we can understand and control it, which makes life easier for us. Even when we try to define a concept like potential, we do so in a limiting manner.

Instead, we must actively guard against mindlessly accepting what we see at face value. If we see anything as unchangeable, innate or the final truth, we limit our potential and that of the world around us.

Biases and labels are ways in which we very easily limit our potential and that of others. Like worldviews, biases and labels are a natural coping mechanism. We need to make sense of a complex world, and it is easier for our brains to do so if we stereotype people and place them in broad categories. Biases and labels limit the factors which we need to consider when we think of a situation, person or scenario. They are convenient, but they are ultimately not necessarily true or useful. The map is not the territory.

For example, we as leaders often use psychological assessment tools to understand and make decisions about people and their careers. However, we must understand what the results of these assessments mean in a systemic context. Even the best assessment tools only assess a dimension of an individual at the specific point at which the assessment is done.

If assessment results expand a person's perception of their abilities, it can open up a new world for that person. However, if we do not understand what the assessment results mean, it can be severely limiting. No assessment result is fixed, whether it measures intelligence, personality or any other aspect of being. We can grow and develop ourselves. Our identities are not fixed.

They evolve over time as we gain experience.

If we blindly use assessment results to label ourselves or others, we limit us and them. We see our identities as fixed, so we make decisions that limit our careers and others' instead of seeking out opportunities that will challenge us to grow and develop.

For this reason, I intentionally avoid the concept of personality as an executive coach. People often say to me, "It's part of my personality", implying that they cannot or do not have to take responsibility for it. This type of thinking often inhibits growth and breakthrough.

Explaining the results of assessments is especially important because most people blindly believe what experts say. Even senior leaders often tell me that nobody ever took the time to explain their assessment results to them in a way that showed them what they mean for them while they have full access to the results. As leaders, we have the responsibility not only to question any limits placed on us, but also encourage those we lead to do the same.

I often see the pain of the prisons people find themselves in because of their limited understanding, previous life experiences, the labels others placed on them or insights that were not shared with them. For example, when I share what assessment results really mean or if I simply act as a sounding board so that people can find more clarity, I see their eyes light up and their energy increase. They become excited about life and what their careers can become when they grasp their unlimited potential.

As individuals, we have specific strengths in our design which we need to focus on. Again and again, I have seen what research has found, i.e., that, "People have several times more potential for growth when they invest energy in developing their strengths instead of correcting their deficiencies".[28] We need to put strategies in place to deal with the areas outside our areas of strength, but our focus should be on our strengths.

Thoughts, words and actions

The ways in which we limit potential, often without being aware of it, manifest in our thoughts, words and actions.

As leaders, we therefore need to be very aware of our thinking and the words which follow from it. Because we create or destroy through the language we use, every word counts. If we think in limiting ways, we will use limiting words or act in limiting ways and set limits on ourselves, our organisations and the people we lead.

To unlock our infinite potential and live life to the fullest, I agree with Robin Sharma that you should only allow the best information to enter.[29] We cannot afford the luxury of negative thought.

Positive mind management is essential for life management. As the Dalai Lama put it, "Watch your thoughts as they become your words; watch your words as they lead to action; watch your acts, as they become habits; watch your habits, as they forge your character; watch your character: it is your destiny".

I find solitude, reflection, prayer and meditation especially useful to become aware of any limiting thoughts and words and to replace them with empowering ones. The use of a coach or a trusted advisor as a sounding board also helps tremendously to make us more aware of our thinking and the words we use.

This process starts with ourselves, circles out to how we deal with others and finally manifests in the future we are creating right now.

Learning from feedback

The reality is that we will not always get it right. We do have limiting thoughts and beliefs. Despite our efforts to become aware of our limits and get rid of them, we will remain unaware of most of them.

That is why feedback is so valuable. Larger systems such as organisations or societies benefit from open feedback, as discussed in Chapter 1.

But as individuals, we benefit from it too. All outcomes are simply feedback loops which offer us opportunities for growth. Success, failures and even disappointments are all part of life, and they all have one thing in common: they are learning opportunities.

If we get positive outcomes, in other words, success, we can build on that. We can consider what we did that contributed to that success and build on it.

We also need to consider the environment or system which allowed that positive outcome to build towards more success, maybe even despite our actions. As Warren Buffet put it, "The boat is more important than the rowing".[30] In other words, a good managerial record as measured by financial returns is far more a function of what business boat you get into than it is of how effectively you rowed, or managed. In fact, it is almost never this or that but rather both.

If we get negative outcomes, such as failures and disappointments, we can also learn from them. Perhaps we can do something differently. Perhaps our assessment of reality was not correct. Perhaps we simply need to learn to persist.

It is much easier to learn from both positive and negative outcomes if we do not attach our value (or that of others) to our results. Results are just that – results. They are a consequence of our actions, *not who we are*. Our value does not lie in our behaviour. It lies in our identity – who we are.

A much more useful way to think of ourselves (and others) is that we are inherently valuable as people. Our behaviour, on the other hand, can and should always improve and it is a life-long journey.

Leading a meaningful life

Acknowledging, noticing and pursuing infinite possibilities is inherently meaningful and exciting. We are creative. We are allowing our unlimited potential to be realised.

We add another layer of meaning to our lives if we also allow others to realise their unlimited potential in pursuit of infinite possibilities. We enhance our own meaning when we help others live meaningful lives too.

Living this way creates more possibilities and more potential. The happy by-product is that it leads to better and more sustainable results for all.

A quote that has inspired me over many years says, "We narrow down the possibilities in our lives by having an extremely limited awareness of our true potential, which is, for all practical purposes, unlimited".[31]

I therefore make a point of starting every day preparing for the best with an expectation that something great can and will happen. Grounded in my inner source, the belief that there is so much more fires me up and propels me forward every day.

Questions for reflection

Before proceeding, take some time to reflect on these questions:

- How much do I see opportunities in the richness of systemic resources that cannot be limited by predicting future results?

- What does infinite possibilities mean for me?

- How do I take others with me to the benefit of both?

- Do I invite feedback from others on a regular basis?

Chapter 6

Clarity of direction

❖

An informal definition of leading is that you're taking people from here to there on a journey. It implies that we need to know where *there* is and where the starting point is for us and the people we're leading. It's about clarity of direction, the fourth leadership dimension and the last one that focuses on the leader's full potential as reflected in the vertical oval of the model.

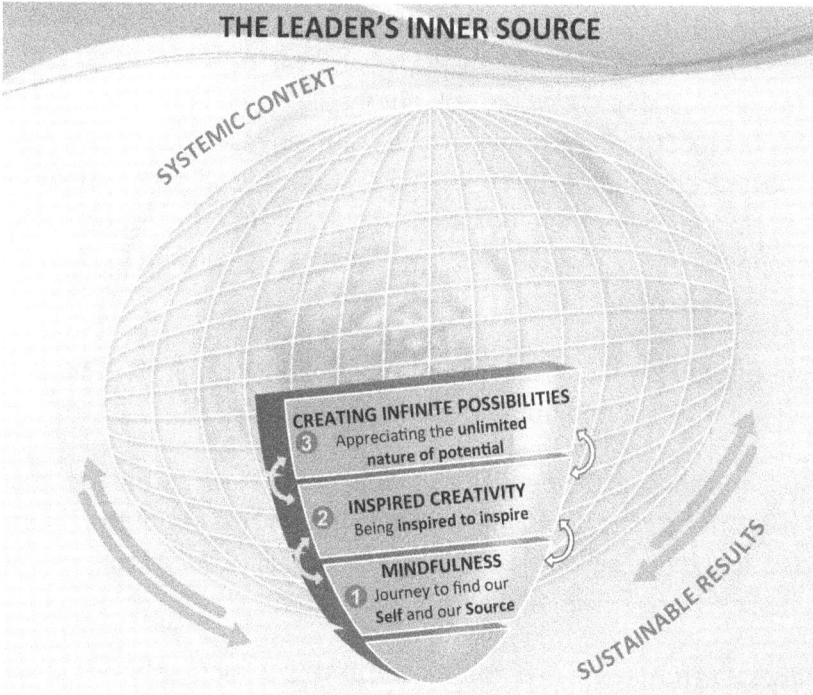

THE LEADER'S INNER SOURCE

SYSTEMIC CONTEXT

CREATING INFINITE POSSIBILITIES
③ Appreciating the unlimited nature of potential

INSPIRED CREATIVITY
② Being inspired to inspire

MINDFULNESS
① Journey to find our Self and our Source

SUSTAINABLE RESULTS

A personal example

As for most people, the year 2020 had a profound impact on how my wife Trudie and I work. Trudie's career is in healthcare, so the pandemic meant more work under more stressful conditions. The biggest change for me was the shift to remote work. I did a fair share of work remotely already, especially with my clients outside South Africa. But suddenly, everything was online, even facilitated team interactions.

As society started opening up again, a big portion of my work continued happening online. For instance, instead of waiting for a chance to meet in person, I could have conversations quicker. While I still prioritise building personal relationships in person, I decided to embrace it as an enabler.

My increased flexibility coupled with Trudie's increased stress and changing family dynamics reignited a vision that had started 20 years ago: to move to West Coast of South Africa. So appealing and so clear was the vision that we decided to take action.

We decided that we would sell our family home in Pretoria, buy a smaller place in Pretoria and move our main residence to the West Coast close to Cape Town. We had made several other attempts to buy a property there before. Three years after the last offer, the property we really wanted was back on the market, and everything fell in place.

We packed up the house in which we had lived for 18 years and settled into not one but two smaller homes.

Trudie also had to identify and onboard a new partner so that she could detach from her practice one week a month. Things developed quickly and we decided that quality of life is important and she stopped working.

Our dream house along the West Coast is a happy place that we have been praying for over the past 20 years. It's a place where we can spend time together experiencing the beauty of nature. We wake up smelling the clean sea air, walk along the beach in quietness and conversation. We have more control of our days and time to spend with each other and in prayer and solitude.

Initially the plan was to spend three weeks a month in Pretoria and one week in the Western Cape. Trudie would get to unplug for a week each month, and I would be able to continue work as normal – and possibly even make new connections in the Cape Town area.

More than a year in, living our vision has turned out so well that, depending on my travelling schedule, we're at the West Coast for two to three weeks during most months. A few special clients (and our grandchild) keep us coming back to Pretoria at least one week a month, though.

Our personal inspired vision evolved over many years with several attempts to buy a property on the West Coast. When it eventually materialised, it was as if everything just came together. What was fascinating was that our oldest daughter who was staying with us in Pretoria was married on the day our West Coast property registered. It marked the end of a great season and the start of an exciting new one.

In most organisational contexts, clarity of direction will likely involve more role players than our story, and the stakes will be higher. But the principles are the same.

Being able to have and provide clarity of direction requires three things: having a clear inspired vision, sharing it with others and acting optimally in the present to realise the vision.

An inspired vision

To have a clear vision, a leader must be able to imagine a clear picture of the future.

In our personal situation, we had been visiting the West Coast for over 20 years. During that time, we were able to enjoy the sound of the waves, the smell of the sea, the freedom of being on a boat or rowing in the waves, the times of solitude and prayer while canoeing or walking on the long beaches untouched by people, the times Trudie and I could spend in conversation and the times spent together as a family. The Wild West, as someone calls the area, grew on us over 20 years.

When it came time for us to make the change, we had a very tangible vision of what the future would be.

A clear vision extends beyond the cognitive i.e., what we can rationally foresee will happen. When we think about the future using only our rational minds, we must take into account all the possibilities of what can happen. The result of rational foresight tends to be risk management and a plan to create the future as opposed to vision.

However, if we look at the future with our rational minds as well as inspired creativity, we look at it differently. We see infinite possibilities.

Infinite possibilities are only part of a vision. We must combine those possibilities with mindfulness – an awareness of our self and our Source. Once we do that, we get a personal, inspired picture of the future in terms of our purpose. We know which future to pursue because it is the most meaningful one which we can help to create. It is the means through which we make a difference in the world around us.

With spiritual insight and inspiration, our vision becomes more than just a possible future. It encompasses our calling – what we are meant to do in life – and gives us ultimate meaning.

When we decided to move to the West Coast, for example, I also sensed on a more spiritual level that this change would give me the space to continue in my personal calling. From an early age, I wanted to make an impact through influencing leaders. One key dimension of my vision in facilitating leadership development is to create an awareness of their spiritual selves. My personal slogan captures my vision: facilitating leadership clarity.

Moving to the West Coast was not retiring. It was the next step in my journey which allowed me to continue to facilitate the development of leaders and help them make a global impact. At the same time, it gives me more time for reflection so that I can share what I have learned in my blogs and newsletter – and this book – and to be able to support the leaders I work with even better.

An inspired vision, whether personal or not, has a conviction to it which lies far deeper than what we can understand with our rational minds. A true vision is beyond the leader's self. There can be a spiritual component to it if we allow it.

A shared vision

An inspired, clear vision is one of the most valuable contributions a leader can make. It is how you inspire others.

The seed for a vision is always in an individual who then brings it to a larger group to fulfil. This picture of the future is what unleashes your creativity and that of others. It fosters higher commitment and productivity. Because leaders often see further into the future with more clarity than most others, they can give hope to everyone around them.

As leaders, our role is to create and uphold an organisational vision that adheres to all the requirements of a personal vision. If your personal vision and that of your organisation are not aligned, it will be a challenge. At a minimum, they must be mutually compatible and re-inforce each other.

The vision of your sphere of leadership must elicit a sense of calling in you and those you lead. Everyone must feel that they are valued, that their lives have meaning and that they are making a difference in the pursuit of this vision. It is the tool through which we can maximise human well-being, corporate social responsibility and organisational performance at the expense of no-one.

Sharing a vision is not a once-off exercise. The ideal future of an organisation or team, as well as the plan of how to get there, must be continuously communicated to all concerned. The vision is made clear and understandable as it is discussed, applied and actioned. Buy-in increases as people start to grasp what that vision truly means for them and others. Whether it is your personal vision or that of your organisation or team, it needs to remain front and centre of every action to stay alive.

Optimal now

Clear direction is about much more than vision. A clear vision only provides clarity on the destination – clear direction includes a plan on how to get there. It starts with knowing which next step to take, something that happens moment by moment in the present.

Some leaders thrive on vision. Whether those they lead get it or not, their minds are always off into the future. They focus less on their current reality.

While our current reality should not limit us, we cannot ignore the present. It is from the present that we create the future. Our vision is evolving, and it will not become real if we do not move towards it from the present.

For that reason, successful leaders know how to detach from the future to be present in the moment. They can compartmentalise events around them which enhances their focus on the now. This enables them to deal with multiple events now without becoming overwhelmed.

The vision is where we are heading. The present is where we must take our next step. It is where we deal with the challenges of our daily lives. It is also where we make a difference in others' lives. Those we lead not only need us to provide them with an inspiring vision; they need us to model and give guidance on how to start making that vision a reality today.

Being present and attuned to the now and having clarity on the next step requires mindfulness. Daily, we need to get rid of the noise of yesterday and detach from the anxiety of the unknown future.

Personally, I aim to prepare myself daily in solitude through reflection and prayer. It is in these moments where I get clarity and guidance for the day ahead.

Guidance often comes in the form of key actions I know I should take that day aside from my usual work. These actions do not have to be big. It can be as simple as calling a specific person, sending an email to someone, hugging your spouse, saying something to your child or acknowledging a piece of work by an employee.

Over time, such actions make a difference. Two inspired actions daily lead to more than 700 actions a year, with compounding benefits.

Living the vision now

So-called visionary leaders sometimes fail to live up to the ideals of their vision. In pursuit of a noble vision, they often defy everything that vision stands for. Such behaviour breaks trust and creates confusion.

The end does not justify the means. How you achieve your vision and how you inspire others through your vision determines the nature of that vision. The people you lead know it intuitively.

To provide clear direction, leaders must live true to their values. They must know what they stand for and uphold it. Their values must be about more than meeting their selfish needs but about providing ethical and unselfish guidance. Leaders cannot fake it; others will see.

A leader must therefore be authentic and lead with integrity.

Authenticity is about being true in being. Integrity, which flows from it, simply means walking the talk, doing what you say you will and being true to what you say you stand for. It gives people the choice of whether they want to join you on this journey.

Both Prathiba and Sibu are excellent examples of this kind of leadership. Prathiba's mission to end world hunger and Sibu's to provide more people with employment come from who they are as people. No matter what the situation, they act in accordance with their ideals.

For instance, as much as Prathiba believes in sustainability, she is not starting or acquiring a company that produces whatever food produce is perceived to be the latest in green living in the developed world. Instead, she is turning her efforts into seeing how to produce sustainable food for those dying of hunger in the developing world.

When Sibu and his team are assessing a strategic venture, he makes it explicit that they need to weigh up the potential for profit and job creation against the risk of layoffs if the venture is not well thought through and ends up being unsuccessful. He is consistent in his drive to prioritise both profit and people.

Authenticity and integrity build trust and create clarity. They also open the door for you to affirm and teach others, increasing your influence for the greater good.

Providing clear direction hinges on taking responsibility and being accountable. Too many leaders blame shift and scapegoat. These behaviours undermine a leader's credibility. People know the truth, even if you try to ignore it.

If a negative result is because of your mistakes and shortcomings, take personal responsibility for it. Remember, results are simply feedback. It is an opportunity to learn and grow.

If you model this behaviour, those you lead will have more confidence to own their mistakes and shortcomings too, which is crucial for their personal growth as well as for the organisation or team to improve and reach its ultimate vision.

Even if you were not personally responsible for a negative result, as the leader, you are still ultimately accountable. Blaming others in such situations is just as destructive for them as it is for you. As the leader, you are responsible for creating and maintaining the right environment for everyone around you to play their role.

One of my long-time business partners used to say that we do not get bad employees, only bad managerial leaders. The leaders are the ones who wrongly recruit employees for a role that does not fit them. It's also the leader who must ensure that they are trained adequately, give them feedback so that they can learn and grow, or move them to a more suitable role. If all else fails, the leader is also responsible for letting such people go.

For the leader, the cause of a problem is never others. It always starts with the leader in the context of the system in which they operate. Leaders who model accountability and responsibility avoid wasting precious energy on confusion. Instead, they create clarity of direction and thus free up their own and others' energy to start creating their ideal future now.

Question for reflection

Before you proceed, reflect on these questions:

- Do I have a clear and inspired vision?

- How well do I detach from my vision to focus on what I can control now?

- What short slogan best captures the vision of what I want to achieve as a leader? (Use as few words as possible, preferably something short and sweet, like *Just Do It* from Nike.)

SECTION 3

THE LEADER'S RELATIONSHIPS

❖

Leadership is about people, so it's not surprising that two of the seven leadership dimensions are about relationships. We are leaders because of the people who follow us.

The fifth and sixth dimensions, unconditional engagement and humane connectivity, make up the horizontal oval in the leadership framework below. They are what gives your leadership wings, so to speak. With other people on board, we can go higher and further than we could have on our own. We can achieve more.

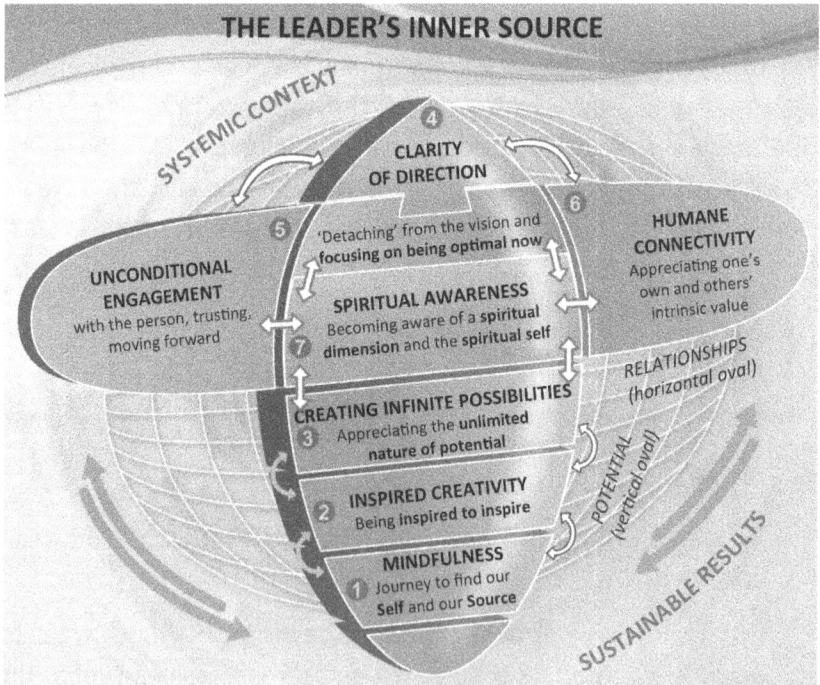

THE LEADER'S INNER SOURCE

SYSTEMIC CONTEXT

4 CLARITY OF DIRECTION

5 'Detaching' from the vision and focusing on being optimal now

6 HUMANE CONNECTIVITY
Appreciating one's own and others' intrinsic value

UNCONDITIONAL ENGAGEMENT
with the person, trusting, moving forward

SPIRITUAL AWARENESS
Becoming aware of a spiritual dimension and the spiritual self

7

RELATIONSHIPS (horizontal oval)

3 CREATING INFINITE POSSIBILITIES
Appreciating the unlimited nature of potential

2 INSPIRED CREATIVITY
Being inspired to inspire

POTENTIAL (vertical oval)

1 MINDFULNESS
Journey to find our Self and our Source

SUSTAINABLE RESULTS

The previous four dimensions that focus on the leader's potential already implied the importance of relationships with others. Leaders are rarely lone heroes who save the day. Instead, they lead the way for others to follow. How we see others and relate with the people around us is therefore a critical factor that determines the outcome of our leadership.

However, the way we think about leadership, especially in business, is often not congruent with these two relationship dimensions. If we want to be great leaders who achieve sustainable results, we need to reframe our thinking and realign our actions.

Chapter 7

Unconditional engagement

❖

In an organisational context, we often incorrectly assume that we as leaders have the right to demand results from those we lead because they are employees. They get paid for their work, after all.

But research has shown that that assumption is not true. "[P]eople are hardwired to resist coercion and to retaliate when they feel manipulated."[32] Instead, it was found that leaders are "accepted or rejected on the strength of their perceived interest in the wellbeing of their employees. Trust is granted or withheld, leadership is seen to be worthy of support or not, primarily on this basis".[33]

If we want to achieve more than what we can as an individual, which is true for every leader, we need to have our people on board. And doing so requires the fifth leadership dimension, unconditional engagement. In other words, we need to show genuine concern for people as human beings.

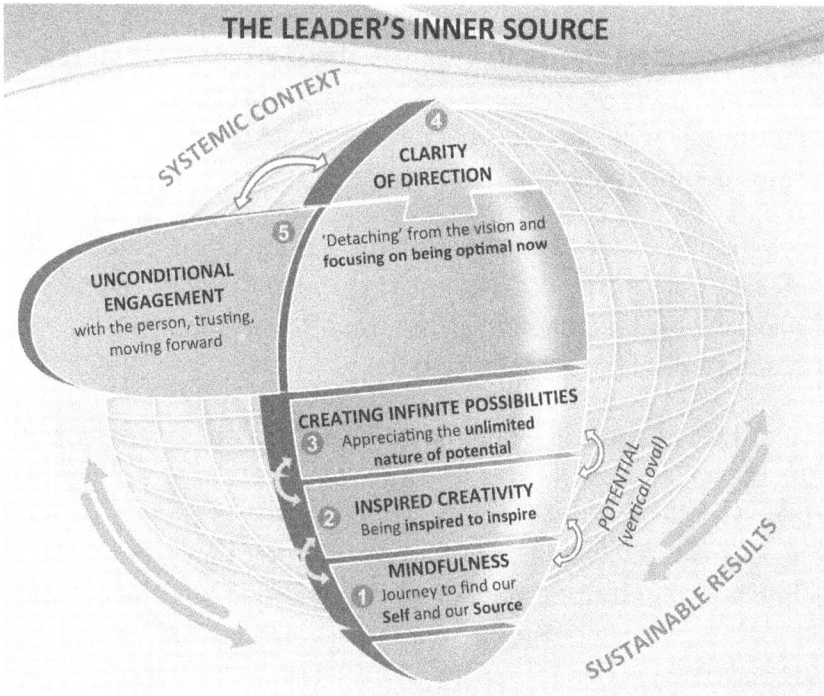

THE LEADER'S INNER SOURCE

SYSTEMIC CONTEXT

④ CLARITY OF DIRECTION

⑤ 'Detaching' from the vision and focusing on being optimal now

UNCONDITIONAL ENGAGEMENT with the person, trusting, moving forward

CREATING INFINITE POSSIBILITIES
③ Appreciating the unlimited nature of potential

② INSPIRED CREATIVITY
Being inspired to inspire

MINDFULNESS
① Journey to find our Self and our Source

POTENTIAL (vertical oval)

SUSTAINABLE RESULTS

The nature of unconditional engagement

Unconditional engagement is about unconditional acceptance of ourselves and others as people. It is about appreciating our own and others' value as intrinsic; in other words, inherent to us as humans, and not based on our behaviours, beliefs or any aspect of ourselves which we relate to our identity.

Unconditional engagement allows us to let go of our desire to be in control and to be right as it relates to another person. It is about what the other person needs, not only about our ideas.

It opens the door for us to trust others more instead of relying solely on ourselves. Because we know that we make mistakes and others do too, we can forgive ourselves and others more easily and quickly. Forgiveness, in turn, allows us to focus on moving forward instead of holding onto past hurts and wrongs.

Parikh calls unconditional engagement "beyond ego".[34] Our egos refer to our own needs and wants – the selfish part of ourselves. When we go beyond our egos, we look beyond ourselves. We humbly ask how we can channel our "ego (energy) to make a contribution out there".[35]

Even though unconditional engagement is about the other person and not our needs, it does not only benefit the other person. Unconditional engagement allows opportunities to come our way because we are open to noticing them.

It also helps us to collaborate towards agreed outcomes: because our ego does not get in the way, everyone can work together towards the same goal. On a personal level, unconditional engagement allows us to experience the joy that can be found in relationships, not only in our work but also in our private lives.

Separating the person from the behaviour

To many people, and leaders in particular, unconditional engagement may sound like a lofty ideal which is simply not possible in practice. Leaders feel that they need to see people for who they are, including the good but also the bad and the ugly.

Unconditional engagement does not require you to ignore all the negative behaviours or differences between you and other people. However, it does require you to separate the person from their behaviour.

Separating the person from the behaviour is about seeing every person as inherently valuable as a human being, as I have mentioned earlier in this chapter. We recognise, accept and value every person simply because they are human, just like us.

For those of us who believe that we are created beings, we see the hand of the Creator in every person as we see it in ourselves. To paraphrase the Golden Rule, we love others as we love ourselves.

Of course, this assumes you love, or value, yourself. The way you love yourself or not limits how you can love others. The same is true with personal development. My colleagues and I see again and again that leaders who don't prioritise their own development do not necessarily see the development of others as that important. Separating the person from the behaviour only applies when you have a healthy sense of self.

When we separate the person from the behaviour, we can suspend all our judgement when we engage with them. We are dealing with the person, and our judgement has no place here.

We simply see the person for who they are, and we unconditionally accept that person as a human being. Doing so enables us to connect with that person exactly where they are. We can focus on their needs, recognise their passions and build a relationship on that foundation.

In my context, whether I am working with a person with exceptional talent in the UK, a great leader in Saudi Arabia or a tracker in the bush in Africa, each of them is a person whom I care deeply about.

The person's behaviour and beliefs are entirely separate from their personhood. We may disagree with what they do or believe. We may even take action against those things. But the way that we do it will be different because we are operating from a place of valuing and caring about the person.

A great mentor of mine, the late Dr David Hendry, often related the story of how he worked in prisons in the United States. As a psychologist, he had to work with long-term prisoners who had done terrible deeds. Those things they had done had become their identity. "You could see evil in their eyes", he used to say.

To find a way to engage with these prisoners, he used the metaphor of a cup and saucer. Even though we use them together, they are two items which we can separate. In his analogy, he saw the saucer to be the person and the relationship with the person, which is always sacrosanct. Their behaviour, paradigms, worldviews and even their culture or race are represented by the cup.

Dr Hendry used to say that you need to separate the cup and the saucer to build an unconditional relationship with the person before anything else. If the relationship between two people is good, you can deal with the differences and even have tough conversations which will not be taken personally. However, if there is no respect for the person and no relationship, even the smallest challenge is difficult to deal with.

People often say or imply that if we do not accept their views and behaviour, we are rejecting them as a person. In my view, that is manipulation, even though they do not necessarily intend it to be.

Our behaviour manifests what we believe about the world, and that is different for all of us. I cannot tell someone to accept my behaviour unconditionally because then I require them to accept my views of what is right and wrong. Doing so is futile – people will believe what they believe. It also denies them the very freedom that I insist they offer me.

It is far more productive to put the behaviour and the underlying beliefs aside. From a place of mutual respect for each other's value as a person, we can then build a relationship and have productive conversations about the rest.

Unconditional engagement does not mean that any behaviour goes. As leaders, we have to set clear boundaries of which behaviour is acceptable and which is not. Organisations, countries and families all benefit from having boundaries for what is acceptable and what is not. If anyone crosses those boundaries, they should understand that there are consequences. However, the consequences deal with the behaviour, not the person.

Unfortunately, separating the person and the behaviour is not standard practice in our society. When working with leadership teams, our team often ask them, "What do you see when you meet a person for the first time?" Usually, their answers show that people tend to be very guarded, critical and judgemental upon the first impression. They focus on the other person's differences in behaviour, culture, gender, race, income, etc. They look for some common ground or some potential to make a connection with others. In the process, they exclude many potentially enriching relationships.

Only very seldom do people say that they see a person who is another human being and that they have an exciting opportunity to get to know that person as someone who exceeds all the stereotypes and labels we impose on them.

A healthy sense of self

The reason unconditional engagement is not common practice comes down to ourselves, our paradigms, our culture – what we believe and how we view ourselves relative to others.

We do unto others what we do unto ourselves. We do not value other people inherently because we do not always see ourselves as intrinsically valuable. We attach our value to our behaviour and successes or failures. We find our identity in our views, ideologies, religion and even in our culture or race.

None of these is wrong, but we cannot find security in them. Those are just things and concepts; they are not us. Even if we let go or change all those things, in essence, we are humans.

Recognising our views as just that, our views, is very freeing. It frees us to accept ourselves and others unconditionally. We can love ourselves and others based on that unconditional acceptance. We can see ourselves and others as people with unlimited potential who can grow and develop.

We can also hold ourselves and others accountable for where we have gotten it wrong in terms of agreed boundaries without any negative emotional consequences. We are freed from fear and our egos because we know our value does not lie in our behaviour, performance or beliefs. Even if we might differ with regards to opportunities, talents or our seniority in an organisation, we are all equal in value as people.

Leaders who can appreciate their intrinsic value can appreciate that of others too. It gives them the ability to treasure relationships, look at others with more empathy and create a safe environment where those they lead can genuinely engage with each other and their work.

Leadership practices

The challenge for many of us is that unconditional engagement is countercultural. Even if it's not, it's far from easy to practice.

Here are some ideas of how to demonstrate and facilitate unconditional engagement in an organisational context:

- **Give unconditionally** without manipulation or expecting a return. Authentic engagement shuts down when employees sense that they are being manipulated or when conditions are attached to their employer's generosity.

- **Let go of historical baggage** to promote the idea that all experiences, both successes and failures, are life lessons. By taking on this constructive perspective of the past, leaders avoid resentment and instead engage unconditionally with other people in co-creating a future of sustainability.

- Be humble enough to **admit mistakes and ask for forgiveness**. In doing so, you create a safe space for employees to take creative chances, even at the risk of failure. A 13-year research study by Dr Brené Brown concluded that there is no innovation and creativity without failure and that vulnerability is the birthplace of human connection and engagement.[36]

- **Let go of the illusion of perfection.** Striving to do better all the time is healthy, but perfectionism destroys the self, creativity, innovation and engagement.

- **Forgive** in a personal and organisational context. We all make mistakes, and organisational life is unbearable if there is no place for forgiveness.

- Let go of the **need to control**. It empowers employees and leads to a more confident and content workforce. Managers can control systems and processes, not people. Leaders lead people, and *the only person leaders need to and can control is themselves*. Forcing people only leads to discontent and discourages them from being creative, effective and productive.

- **Appreciate, respect and trust employees' judgements** and allow them to be proactive. It is a vote of confidence, a sign of respect and opens the door to unconditional engagement and the creation of new opportunities.

- **Value the importance of collaboration** to reach a common purpose and to achieve sustainable results. Focus on what others need, value them and build on their contributions, listen carefully, acknowledge and support the success of others, and encourage open conversations.

- **Hold yourself and others accountable** for what you agree and commit to do.

Unconditional engagement in practice

Unconditional engagement is not soft and fluffy – it takes courage. It is a crucial skill for all leaders and managers who want their teams to operate effectively to reach organisational goals. We can only display this dimension if we are mature with a healthy sense of self, and if we've learnt to separate the person from their behaviour.

Hugo, the HR leader I introduced at the start of this book, showed some remarkable growth in this dimension during the time that I coached him.

As I referred to before, when the head of HR ignored him in a corporate setting, it really upset him. As a nice but sometimes insecure person, his first instinct was that he must have upset or angered her. But he couldn't think of what he had done. And she hadn't mentioned anything either.

When we discussed what happened in our coaching session, he vented his feelings for a long time. Often, that is the best thing to do in a safe space like that. Eventually, with not much prodding from my side, he started suggesting alternative reasons. He realised that her actions might not have had anything to do with him but with the bigger context in which they operated.

He admitted that he found it hard to imagine that not everyone thinks and is motivated the same way he is. He especially tends to expect his superiors to always act in the most pure moral ways, and he is often taken by surprise when they don't.

His realisation was that he instead of jumping to conclusions, he should take time to reflect. Even if what he observes doesn't make sense and even seems wrong in his eyes, the best approach is to not take it personally and to accept that that behaviour made sense to that person in the moment.

Understanding unconditional engagement, interestingly, made him less naïve. Instead of figuring out who and what is right and wrong and seeing everything as a matter of white and black, he increasingly became aware of all the shades of grey that are often at play in organisations at higher levels. Realising that his own motives are often just as complicated from the outside for others made him more humble too.

I commended Hugo for coming to these realisations as it relates to his superiors. However, they are as applicable to peers and direct reports. Leaders often ask me how to handle situations where direct reports or even peers are out of line. If you consider the complexity that diversity in terms of cognition, behaviours, styles age, gender, culture or race can bring to these situations, it's not surprising that many people simply avoid them.

My best advice for navigating this maze of labels is to engage with the person unconditionally and deal with the behaviour separately.

Questions for reflection

- How do I look at people when I meet them? Do I see a person first and foremost before I notice their physical appearance, how they dress or their facial expression, or do I look for signs to confirm whether they will bring value to me?

- Do I have more grace or more criticism? Which way has this balance shifted as I have grown older?

- If I need to address out-of-line behaviour, can I separate the person from the behaviour?

- How difficult is it for me to separate the person from the behaviour when I need to forgive someone? Are there any people I need to forgive?

Chapter 8

Humane connectivity

❖

When it comes to the "soft skills" of relationships in organisations, standard practice and best practice are very much out of alignment. Research has shown and practice has proven that the most successful leaders and organisations care about their people and enable them.

And yet, caring about its people is not the status quo at most organisations.

The result is that only 21% of the workforce are engaged.[37] And if you're a manager, your situation is likely worse: managers report higher stress and burnout than the people they manage.[38]

In the words of Gallup's CEO and Chairperson, Jim Clifton, "The practice of management really is broken".[39]

The sixth leadership dimension, humane connectivity, is the antidote to this crisis in leadership. Humane connectivity is generated in relationships. It is about appreciating our own and others' intrinsic value, fostering quality relationships and caring for others.

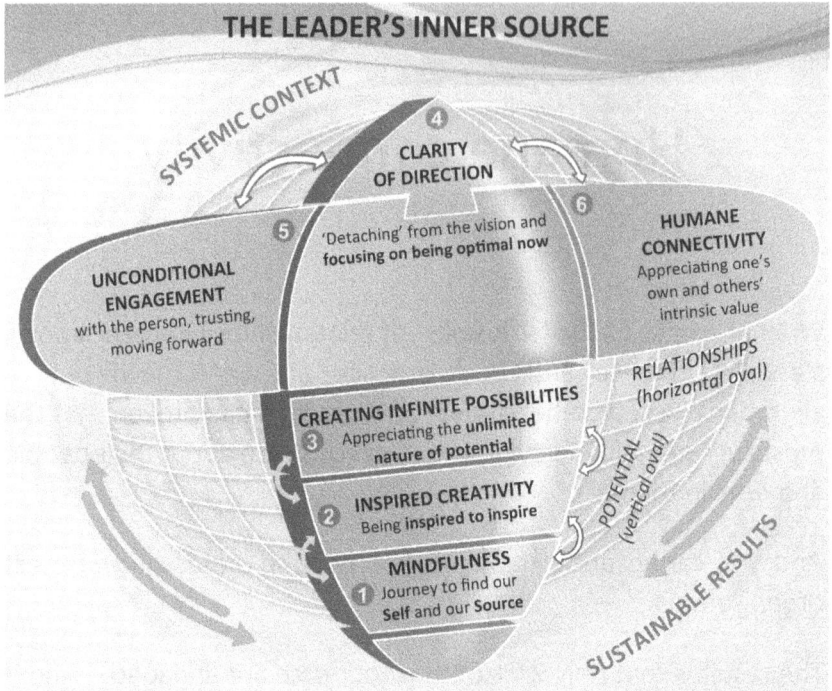

THE LEADER'S INNER SOURCE

The two cornerstones of humane connectivity – appreciation and care – are often incorrectly seen as nice things to do instead of what they are important ingredients to personal and organisational success.

Martin Luther King Jr said, "It really boils down to this: that all life is interrelated. We are all caught in an inescapable network of mutuality, tied into a single garment of destiny. Whatever affects one destiny, affects all indirectly".

All of us are connected to others, but it is our choice whether we want to make our connections humane.

Why leaders must care

If standard management practice that focuses on directing and administrating has resulted in a disengaged workforce and burnout managements, what's the alternative?

Gallup's research offers some clues.[40] They have found that "great management is [...] not [about] directing and administrating". Instead, great management is "an act of coaching".

Gallup's meta-analysis of 100 million employee interviews produced a breakthrough finding: "a full 70% of the variance between highest engaged teams and persistently disengaged teams is *just the manager*" (their emphasis).

Legitimate Leadership, one of the organisations with which I partner, has found exactly the same.

Their work is based on research done in the South African gold mining industry in the late 1980s. Despite times of great racial, political and economic tension, not politics, race, physical conditions, rates of pay or the presence of a union was found to be determining factors of good employer-employee relations and productivity.

The only factor was managers.

Specifically, they found the distinguishing factor to be whether managers have a genuine concern for their people as human beings and whether managers enable their people to realise the best in themselves.

As Wendy Lambourne puts it in the book *Legitimate Leadership*, "Care and growth [...] make the power which is exercised by those in authority legitimate".[41]

Employees will only be willing and productive workers if they know those who lead them genuinely care and therefore enable their growth as much as that of the organisation.

Without genuine care, it all falls flat, and you're stuck working with the 80% of the workforce who is disengaged.

Care that demands responsibility and accountability

So what does genuine care look like in an organisational context?

The solution to the traditional management style of command and control suggested by both Gallup and *Legitimate Leadership* is that the manager should become an enabling coach.

Think back to the leaders in your life who inspired you to be who you are today. These people touched you on a deep emotional level. They made a difference in your life because they believed in you and saw something in you that you were not able to see for yourself at the time. They cared.

As an executive coach, I have seen again and again that I must genuinely care about the person I am coaching to be effective. Care cannot be artificial. It must be real, or the other person will know it. You must find a way to care deeply about each individual that affects you and your organisation, as well as the ones that are affected by you.

Coaching must start with genuine care about the person and their world to be effective.

But coaching doesn't stop with caring. It involves so-called *tough love*. People must be held accountable to a high standard of excellence. The results matter.

It's not that the results in and of themselves should not be what ultimately matter to the leader or manager as coach. Instead, tasks and results are important "as the means to enable people".[42]

Like I do with the executive leaders that I coach, the ultimate aim for leaders should be the growth of their people into exceptional human beings. Sustainable results that exceed the standard expectations we have of workers are the happy by-product.

That's not to say that leaders are simply cheerleaders. They must ensure that their teams have the means to deliver what is expected of them. They must also ensure that their people are held accountable for what is within their control.

As Wendy Lambourne explains, "Coaching is an exceptionally useful process for enabling or improving employee contribution but ONLY when the issue affecting contribution is ability, [...] not when either means or accountability issues are at stake".[43]

Love and forgiveness

The type of deep and genuine caring we're taking about here is the essence of love.

I am not talking about romantic love or the bond of friendship or other kinds of relationships that develop because of our level of closeness to the other person. It does not even mean that we need to like the person.

We simply care about people as individuals on a deep and authentic level.

When people talk about loving everyone, they often confuse it with accepting their behaviour. Again, it is important to separate the person and the behaviour. I might disagree completely and even be disgusted by certain behaviour, but I can genuinely care about and therefore love the person.

For example, over the years I have worked with more than one person who was dismissed for unacceptable behaviour. While I agreed with the assessment of their behaviour, I always felt empathy for the person. In some cases, their behaviour was clearly a result of the system in which they functioned.

I was willing to coach these people because I care enough about the person to want to help them get to a point where they behave differently. The only way to support them in doing so is to genuinely care.

I have also been on the receiving end of such situations. Twice in my career I was asked to leave the executive team in entrepreneurial organisations. In one case, it was because of association – I was perceived to be too close to another person who was asked to leave. In the other case, I was accused of practices that I didn't do and was blamed for certain outcomes.

Separating the person from the behaviour also helps to navigate situations like these. Unconditional love keeps no record of wrong. When a person's behaviour affects you negatively, this unconditional love of the person allows us to forgive – in other words, to let go of the hurt and offence and to forget. That does not mean we are saying the behaviour was right. We are simply no longer holding it against that person.

The journey of life is not always easy. Without taking away any responsibility from an individual who wrongs us, we can show care and compassion for the challenges others face when we forgive them. We can look beyond their unacceptable behaviour and care deeply for the person. We can choose to forget.

It's not that we cannot remember the wrong; it's that we choose to remember the better things – the worthy things in life. By doing so, we free ourselves from that hurt and we give the person the freedom to do better in future.

Appreciation

If care is one side of the coin of humane connectivity, appreciation is the other.

While caring, as well as loving and forgiving, are internal, acts of appreciation are a very practical outflow of these foundational concepts.

To appreciate means to recognise something or someone's value. When we recognise, we acknowledge existence. To appreciate, then, is to attach value to someone's existence. We make them feel valuable merely for being themselves.

In *A Theory of Human Motivation*, Abraham Maslow theorised that humans have five basic needs.[44] Esteem, the need for respect and admiration, is one of them. Esteem starts with recognising people's existence and appreciating them for who they are. When we look at people through an appreciative lens, we can identify the positive things that they do and their true potential much more easily and accurately.

Conversely, as Ken Blanchard has said, the ultimate demise of any relationship is when someone does something right, but they do not do it right enough.[45] A lack of appreciation and unrealistic expectations destroy our relationships.

The effects of appreciation on a person are remarkable; they feel that their existence matters. When people feel empowered, they bring more of themselves to a situation and a relationship. Appreciation opens the door for a genuine connection and an authentic relationship.

Appreciation can be shown in as simple an act as knowing and using a person's name. It's a practical way to say to them that they are important enough for me to put in the effort to get to know their name.

An authentic connection requires more than appreciating the other person; it starts with a healthy sense of self-appreciation.

Self-appreciation is not about thinking highly of ourselves or our achievements. It is about knowing that our value is not tied to our behaviour, beliefs or any other attribute. Like other people, we are valuable simply because we are humans. We appreciate ourselves when we recognise the value of our human existence.

From this place of self-appreciation, we can extend appreciation to any person who comes our way.

Relationships as assets

I've mostly spoken about a leader's relationship with those they lead in this chapter. However, humane connection extends to your relationship with any other person. This dimension implies that all relationships are precious assets.

Most leaders acknowledge the importance of networking for their career progression. It comes down to the people you know and have a relationship with who trust and believe in you.

However, many aspiring leaders pursue networking for its own sake. That approach deprives you of the real benefits of networking.

Mutually beneficial relationships turn us into people who can make more valuable contributions. The value is in the person we are becoming and who we help other people to become. We are sowing long-term seeds, not looking for a quick and direct return, even though it can happen.

Keith Ferrazzi, *New York Times* bestselling author and world-renowned speaker, agrees.[46] Based on his success and that of his clients, his company researched the effect of relationships on success. They found that "the number-one predictive element of an individual's success is the number, quality and depth of social capital – the personal relationships among those that they do business with".[47]

Based on their research and experience, Ferrazzi's business, Relationship Masters Academy, therefore shows its clients how to manage their relationships more effectively for greater mutual success.

It all starts with knowing what the key relationships in your life are. It is important to cover all spheres of life: business, family, spiritual, visible and invisible. List the individuals in each of the areas and prioritise them. Include people whom you do not know or who you would like to know better.

Once your list is in place, define what you can do for them.

Some of the simple things that Ferrazzi likes to do for the people on his list is to phone and wish them a happy birthday. Another simple yet significant act is to be interested in people's children. He pays attention when people speak about their personal lives and even jots down details to help him remember them.

Ferrazzi has learnt and teaches his clients to always be on the lookout for ways to connect other people in ways that can benefit all. Even if the direct benefit to him is not clear, he has learnt that his investment in relationships always yields a return.

Part of that return is in the sheer satisfaction of helping another human being. However, it also has direct and powerful results in business that can be measured in financial terms as a return on investment.

He has discovered the power of combined energy when humans are connected to each other.

Prathiba and I have lately been speaking a lot about relationships as assets in our coaching conversations.

Her ambition and mission, combined with an increasingly strong focus on people, have given her a formidable network. Over and above her international business network from her corporate career, and now with her own nationwide business, she has academic connections at Harvard and Oxford as well as a growing political network. For instance, she advises the president of an African country.

To take the next step in her career, she will have to build an even stronger network and leverage it to open the right doors for her. Despite her drive and passion, the fact that she is a non-white Muslim women is, sadly, still making it hard for her to have influence in certain circles.

Prathiba has come far enough in her career to realise that she can't pursue relationships in a mercenary fashion. She must build humane engagements and find a way to align with different people via beliefs, values or outcomes, as the situation may be.

She does not know how it will happen, but she is confident that the path will emerge step by step, relationship by relationship.

Getting down to the basics

If you reflect on everything that this chapter has covered, the crux of it is that relationships are the basic building blocks of our society.

To use systemic terminology, relationships are the fractals of our societies, organisations and individual lives. They are small, representative aspects of the whole. The nature of our relationships determines that of our societies, organisations and our personal lives.

In that view, building humane connections is a very logical thing to do for everyone. It is a fundamental part of being successful humans.

However, for many people and in many systemic contexts, that is not true. We do not simply build great relationships. We must put time and effort into it. We must have conversations about it. We must learn it. Something as simple and fundamental as a humane connection with another person has become something precious to aspire to.

The reason humane connections are not easy or natural is because of the systems in which we operate.

Early in my career, I worked with long-term prisoners. During that time, I got to know some of them very well. Most of them were not horrible monsters. They were nice people, but they had been operating in a system which they were not able to resist. The final decision to take the actions that led them to prison was theirs, yes. However, if they had not been in that system, they would not have become criminals. In the system in which they operated, they did.

I saw the same effect in some of the people in that prison system even if they were not prisoners. Most of them were also nice people, but some showed extreme levels of violence towards the prisoners and treated them inhumanely in various ways. They stooped to the level of the system in which they functioned. Once, a prisoner almost escaped, and the level of violence towards that person was completely inappropriate.

For both prisoners and those who dealt with them, it was not necessarily the individuals that made dubious decisions. They operated in flawed systems, which led to negative behaviour.

In *The Lucifer Effect*, Philip Zimbardo discusses why and how this happens.

He mentions, for example, "groupthink", the phenomenon that occurs when "all members of an organisation become so inward-looking that they fail to recognise when the assumptions driving their behaviour are false, outmoded, or even self-destructive".[48] However, it is not all bad news. Groups can just as easily design systems and behavioural models that lead to positive actions.

Most leaders do not work in the context of prisons, however I include this extreme example because I have encountered the same phenomenon many times outside those prison walls. We as leaders and those we lead all operate in systems, and too many of our systems deprive us of creating a culture of humane connectivity.

For example, I recently attended a leadership meeting where two people suggested that we should give someone notice and get rid of them. I was surprised as I thought that was a much too extreme reaction to the situation. However, upon reflection, I realised that this was a result of that system, which includes a poor relationship with the person under discussion.

It is therefore vital that we recognise that we operate in systems and what the assumptions of our systems are that drive our behaviours. We must do the same for those we lead, not because we are better than them, but because we know that they are also like us, fallible humans operating in incomplete and broken systems.

Most importantly, we must start creating a more successful path through the way we build relationships. Through appreciation, love and care, we are slowly, fractal by fractal, building new systems where humane connectivity is not the exception but the norm.

The result

Humane connection is clearly very different from what is standard management and leadership practice in many organisations.

It's no wonder that 80% of the worldwide workforce is disengaged and that managers are chronically stressed and burnt out. Our accepted practices are actively sabotaging people's productivity by violating basic principles of human nature and motivation.

That's why humane connectivity is not a nice to have. It has personal and organisational consequences. If the decisions we make and the actions we take as leaders come from a place of humane connectivity, it has a ripple effect.

For example, if employees feel valued and accepted, they extend that caring attitude to their colleagues, customers and other stakeholders like suppliers.

Humane connectivity unleashes the power of growth and development for individuals and organisations. It creates a more humane world for everyone's benefit. And it starts with the person we come into contact with next.

As Maya Angelou famously said, "People will forget what you said, people will forget what you did, but people will never forget how you made them feel".

What excites me is that it *is* possible to change our thinking and actions – and to do so on an organisational level, not only a personal level. As leaders, we have the power to create the enabling environment in our organisations that our people need, which will produce exceptional results sustainably.

Questions for reflection

- How do you connect with others in a humane way and care for the person?

- Can I hold people accountable for their behaviour without breaking the relationship with the person?

- Create a network map: a page with three columns. In the first, write down the names of people you know in a business context. In the second, list the people who will support you. In the third, list the people who believe in you no matter what happens. These are the people who will advocate for you even when you are not present. What does this map mean for your leadership journey?

SECTION 4

THE LEADER'S SPIRIT

❖

The final dimension of the leadership framework, spiritual awareness, focuses on how leaders can become aware of a spiritual dimension and develop their spiritual selves to become well-rounded leaders.

Of all the seven dimensions, spiritual awareness can be the most potent force in our leadership, which is why it lies at the heart of the leadership framework.

However, it can also be the most difficult to access if we are not open to it.

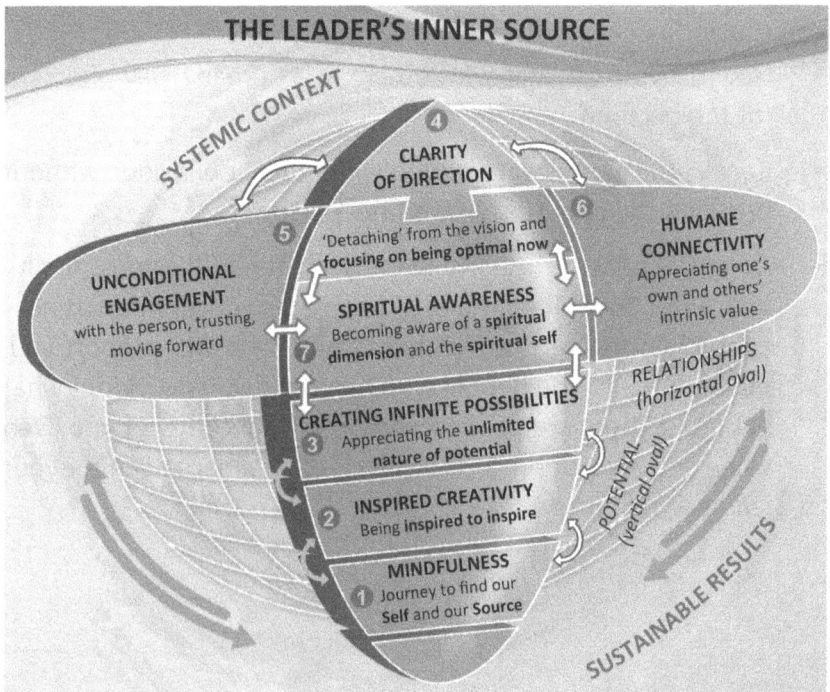

THE LEADER'S INNER SOURCE

SYSTEMIC CONTEXT

4 CLARITY OF DIRECTION

5 'Detaching' from the vision and focusing on being optimal now

6 HUMANE CONNECTIVITY
Appreciating one's own and others' intrinsic value

UNCONDITIONAL ENGAGEMENT
with the person, trusting, moving forward

SPIRITUAL AWARENESS
Becoming aware of a spiritual dimension and the spiritual self

7

RELATIONSHIPS
(horizontal oval)

CREATING INFINITE POSSIBILITIES
3 Appreciating the unlimited nature of potential

POTENTIAL
(vertical oval)

INSPIRED CREATIVITY
2 Being inspired to inspire

MINDFULNESS
1 Journey to find our Self and our Source

SUSTAINABLE RESULTS

Chapter 9

The leader's spirit

❖

"I'm not really a spiritual person", a senior leader recently told me.

I didn't say so at the moment, but I would beg to differ. While many people do not see spirituality as something that influences their daily actions, I believe we are all spiritual people. However, because we have different associations with the word "spiritual", we end up using different words to refer to that part of our lives.

Spiritual awareness is the seventh and final leadership dimension. It sits at the core of the leadership model I developed because it informs all the others.

All leaders can become better by growing this dimension and tapping into their spirituality, whether they use that word to describe it or not.

In this chapter, I explore what spirituality is and why it is important for us as leaders and our organisations. I also discuss how to live out and allow spiritual awareness in our organisations – in a way that does not provoke negative consequences but allows everyone to bring their whole self to their work.

Spirituality defined

Spirituality is a metaphysical concept. It refers to that which is beyond what can be analysed, proven or known through our senses.

Incorporating such metaphysical concepts in business or other secular organisations is often seen as inappropriate. As discussed in Chapter 2, many of the philosophies that shaped our western worldview have no place for spirituality. Some people therefore see it as outdated or as something that should be kept for your personal or religious life.

Recently, however, more and more people have come to question this segmented view of ourselves and have sought how to engage their whole selves in the work environment. Spirituality is important to many of us, and people like Sibu, Prathiba and I find that it plays an integral part in all aspects of our lives.

As mentioned when we discussed the tripartite self in Chapter 2, spirituality is a personal and uniquely individualised construct. It means different things to different people.

Many people have had an experience or thought, or have sensed a voice or a presence that extended beyond their rational minds, will and emotions. We do not tend to think of Charles Darwin as a spiritual person or someone who was spiritually inspired. However, he was able to remember the very place on his journey where he received a sudden moment of inspiration that led to his book, *The Origin of Species*.

Very broadly, the spiritual refers to an unknown realm beyond our selves. People's spirituality often involves a journey of discovery and/or a set of beliefs and practices around this unknown realm. Sometimes it involves a god and sometimes not.

The organisation International Spirit at Work[49] defines spirituality as follows (emphasis mine):

> *a state or experience that can provide individuals with direction, meaning, provide feelings of understanding, support, inner wholeness and/or connectedness.* **Connectedness can be to themselves, other people, nature, the universe, a god, or**

some other supernatural power. The vertical component in spirituality is a desire to transcend the individual ego or personality self. The name put on the vertical component might be God, Spirit, Universe, Higher Power or something else. The horizontal component in spirituality is a desire to be of service to other humans and the planet.

This definition attempts to encapsulate the entire spectrum of what spirituality can mean for different people. On one end, spirituality is equated with emotional intelligence that lies within the self instead of outside it. In other words, it is synonymous with or similar to our soul. On the other end of the spectrum, spirituality is a close, personal relationship with a god or creator, which is a Being separate from oneself.

Each one of our views will lie somewhere along that spectrum.

The benefit of spiritual awareness

Whatever your view of spirituality is, all of us can gain from spiritual awareness.

It's especially important for leaders. In my PhD research[50], all of the 18 senior leaders who were part of the study said that there is a place for spirituality in leadership. Spirituality informs clear values, which help us to provide clarity of direction. Clear values support an inspired vision and keep us on track to live up to that vision in the present.

Sibu has told me, for example, that he gets the strength to face his day by getting down on his knees for prayer every day. People who report to him have also reported that the thing that makes him stand out as a leader the most is his deep spiritual values. He believes in, receives guidance from, and submits to something bigger than himself.

Spiritual awareness can also inform a leader's decision-making. It is a source of wisdom that provides guidance and clarity, which is especially useful in situations that cannot be resolved with reason only.

During coaching, for example, I can have two types of conversation with leaders who are looking for career and business clarity.

During the one type of conversation, the answers are simple. These leaders are clearly not operating in line with their potential, and the steps they should follow in an organisational context are relatively knowable and clear.

But during the other type of conversation, the answer is not simple or obvious. With these leaders, I often reach a point where I honestly do not know what question to ask next. These conversations stretch the limits of the soul, including our cognitive capacity, ambition and emotional insights.

After we have exhausted what is knowable, predictable and linkable using all the optimal thinking and decision-making strategies, we eventually reach a point where what we need next can only be found in the space of the unknowable, that of the spirit.

When we are brave enough to venture into the space of the spirit, the breakthroughs and insights are always tremendous. An international leader I know, for example, recently experienced a lack of clarity. When we had ran out of options to consider in our engagements, she turned to prayer to discern the way forward. Not long after, she achieved a major breakthrough and moved several levels up in her organisation in a short space of time.

As I've mentioned, even though Prathiba is Muslim and I am Christian, she has also asked me more than once to pray for her. When we last spoke about the uncertainty of her path forward, she told me that she had a deep peace about what the next steps will be, even though she doesn't know yet what they will be.

As these examples show, spiritual awareness is a source of passion and purpose which focuses the minds of leaders on making an optimal contribution in their world. Spirituality drives personal growth. It promotes a healthy sense of self and behaviour that is beneficial not only for ourselves, but also for others. Spirituality helps leaders shift their focus away from personal ambition only, to using their abilities and experience for the greater good.

These benefits of spiritual awareness are clearly not only important for leaders. Spiritual awareness ignites a sense of purpose, legacy and meaning in all people. This state of being is important for any person to be wholly engaged in whatever they do. It greatly enhances engagement of the whole person in the workplace, which is important for both leaders and employees.

Several research studies have reported the positive effects of spiritual awareness[51], including:

- better physical and mental health;

- better well-being and life satisfaction;

- higher levels of commitment and engagement;

- practices of care and creativity; and

- improved engagement, problem solving and decision-making.

All these behaviours contribute to a more productive work environment which, in turn, translates into more sustainable business results.

How to practice spiritual awareness

To become spiritually aware or grow our spiritual awareness, we must clarify what we see as our spiritual self and how we develop it. In this section, I offer some ways to do that. These practices, summarised below, emerged from my research, the work of various authors and the incredible leaders I have worked with over many years. They are also ones that I have personally found valuable.

The diagram above shows that spiritual awareness emanates from our spirits. It certainly extends to our souls and our bodies, and the experiences we have with our bodies or souls impact our spirits. However, spiritual awareness, in essence, is about transcending our bodies and souls.

Spiritual awareness starts with access to our Source. When we slow down and spend time in solitude, we can clear ourselves of the day-to-day noise. I find it useful to write things down or to do a mind map of an issue that is on my mind. Many people find meditation to be helpful too. These practices help us clear the clutter in our minds, get to a place of quiet inside of ourselves and be able to listen.

Listening refers to physical listening to the people around us, as well as to spiritual sensing. Being able to "listen" spiritually helps us get clearer perspectives and a sharper awareness of our access to unlimited resources. It also helps us to value others and their passions as well as appreciate their challenges. It illuminates the web of visible and invisible connections to which we have access.

This type of spiritual communication, what we often call "prayer", is two-way. It is about listening and sensing answers, but it is also about expressing what we feel, think and would like to have answers on. It is asking for answers to our difficult questions and expressing our thoughts and feelings. It then transitions to listening for and sensing answers to our questions, receiving clarity of thought and serenity in our emotions.

To practice such a spiritual connection, we need faith. Spiritual practices have an invisible aspect to them, so we need to believe Something or Someone beyond us is there, even though we cannot access it with our senses. Instead of having anxiety about the unknown, we find hope in it.

We can and should, however, use our senses to enhance our access to our Source. We study certain topics or writings. We receive spiritual guidance from others, like mentors, coaches or those in our spiritual communities. Relationships can be seen as sacred for many reasons. A primary reason, for me, is that they allow us to access our Source through such kinds of guidance and feedback.

I find it especially valuable to get feedback from others as sounding boards. People will not simply step into this kind of role, however. We must give them permission to tell us what they experience when they engage with us, including to challenge our established ways of thinking and doing.

The spiritual practices as per the diagram above flow from our connection with our Source. Because our spirit is like a muscle that can and should be developed through practice, we grow spiritually as we live spiritually aware lives. To access the spiritual, we have to be open to it.

No matter what is happening around, with or within us, we can experience a supporting presence. This presence provides rest and a place of healing. We also experience clear purpose and access to the right information at the right time. We have peace about what we are aiming for in life, and we know when to act and when to wait in that pursuit.

Spiritual awareness and religion

Many people equate spirituality with religion. Whether religion has a positive connotation for you or not, viewing the two as the same thing has some pitfalls.

Religion is a difficult term to define, but one way to think of it is as an organised system of beliefs and practices which are shared by a community or group. It usually involves worshipping a god. Put differently, it is an organised means by which people practice spirituality. Not only are there many different religions, but within religions, there are different schools of thought or practice.

The challenge is that religion has different connotations for different people. Some associate it with restriction and control. Others find freedom in it because it offers them a meaningful way to practice their spirituality. Some people have no affinity for religion, yet they have a keen awareness of their spiritual self. Still others see spirituality as inseparable from religion or from *their* religion.

Because of these differences, the topic of religion can be very divisive. Getting involved in religious debates, for example, can be a minefield where everyone walks away a loser.

As a leader, it is important to be aware of these differences when it comes to religion. Start with recognising your associations with religion, whether positive, negative or somewhere in between. Recognise that those feelings and ideas form part of your worldview. Just because you see it that way does not mean that others do too.

Just because religion can be divisive does not mean that you, your employees or your organisation have to be deprived of the benefits of spiritual awareness. Facilitating an environment for divine connection and faith in the workplace is a bold yet necessary and empowering step in pursuit of sustainable results.

Spiritual safety at work

I have touched on the concept of psychological safety in earlier chapters, in other words, where people feel safe enough in a certain context that they participate and contribute without fear of negative consequences to themselves. It is an accepted term in psychology that is often used to talk about contributing at work, for example, when it comes to innovation.

I want to extend this concept of psychological safety to that of spiritual safety. In a spiritually safe environment, we accept people unconditionally while acknowledging that we all need to continue to work on ourselves and our behaviour. A spiritually safe environment also provides a space for all people to experience and practice spiritual connection to their Source with all the benefits that it entails.

A spiritually safe environment opens the door to safety of expression. In most contexts, people do not feel safe to express their views, ask difficult questions or challenge the status quo. Instead, they avoid difficult topics and go with the flow. The unfortunate consequence is that it is difficult, if not impossible, to find solutions to the complex problems posed by our world. We cannot address the underlying causes of our problems because we cannot talk to each other about the most important things in life.

The reason safety of expression is so rare is because separating the person and the behaviour is not common practice. We are afraid or concerned that those around us will be offended or feel rejected if we have different views. Because of these concerns, we are unable to take a firm stance. We operate according to political correctness, which prevents us from changing the status quo, even if the status quo is not desirable or good.

Because of the potential divisiveness of religion and the fear of backlash, organisations exclude and ignore our spirits and our spiritual well-being. Leaders and followers alike are required to operate only as bodies and souls, without bringing our spirits into our work.

Because of the limitations of our souls – in other words, our minds, wills and emotions devoid of spiritual connection and guidance – one of the negative consequences is the prominence of super souls. In business and government alike, too many senior leaders only focus on what they can get out of the system. They operate with hidden agendas and are willing to sacrifice anything or anyone to get what they want. For example, I have seen leaders happily allow a division to fail in their quest for global expansion.

We are not able to forge a different path than that of greed, abuse of power and promoting the agendas of the privileged few without being able to speak the truth in love. I am not suggesting this to be an easy path. Each of us must decide whether we have the courage to do so in the context of our complicated and, at times toxic, global system. Rising above powerful systems is not easy.

Even if it is not easy, I want to encourage you with the fact that we do have that option. Others have chosen this path and are following it courageously and successfully. Instead of a super soul, we can be a different kind of leader who opens up new dimensions and levels of interaction for those around us.

We can accept limitations in ourselves and dependence on something or Someone bigger than ourselves. We have an opportunity to access and engage with the whole person, including our spirts in the work environment. A simple example of how to do it is to create an opportunity at the start of a meeting where everyone can be quiet and access their source in preparation for a meeting. When we have created an opportunity like this, people have used words like "inspired", "ready" and "excited" afterwards.

We can take engagement to a different level of connection by being aware of people's purpose and what kind of meaningful legacy they want to leave behind.

Leadership practices

How you practically live out your spiritual awareness in your leadership context will be different for every person.

To assist you in your journey, I share a few principles and practical ways I and the leaders I engaged with as part of my study have applied:

- Develop your spiritual self through daily solitude, prayer, reflection and meditation to contribute to being a well-rounded leader.

- Demonstrate and model growth and awareness of your spiritual self. Display your personal faith in the workplace and live up to it with a lifestyle of love, no judgement and care.

- Show that you really care about the person by acknowledging and engaging the whole person, including their spiritual self.

- Take a spiritual stance without overstepping the boundaries of others. Talk about what you believe with permission, yet allow others to believe in their construct of their spiritual Source.

- Allow people to pray, meditate and reflect in the workplace to enable their spirits to connect to their Source and grow their spiritual selves.

- Create an environment and culture where individuals focus beyond themselves, spirituality is acknowledged and a spiritual relationship with their Source is encouraged.

- Create a spiritual support structure for employees through regular counselling and consulting opportunities led by spiritual facilitators and coaches. These sessions could be facilitated one-on-one or in a group.

- Record this new culture of spirituality in a policy framework.

If we as leaders grasp the importance of spiritual awareness, it does not mean that everyone around us will too. However, we can open the door for others in our organisations to experience their own spirituality.

Growing our spiritual awareness increases our ability to live out all our other dimensions too. Living and leading this way is how we change our own lives, the lives of those around us, our organisations and our world. We live out our purpose, and we build a better world by doing so – a world that leaves us all the richer.

This verse, attributed to Mother Theresa, sums up the leader's responsibility very well for me:

> *Give the world the best you have, and it may never be enough. Give the world the best you've got anyway. You see, in the final analysis, it is between you and God. It was never between you and them anyway.*

Questions for reflection

Before you proceed, take time to reflect on these questions:

- What is the role of spirituality in my leadership?

- What are some of my spiritual practices?

- Can you see and acknowledge a person beyond their religious labels?

- Am I comfortable enough in my spiritual grounding and journey that I can allow others their space to grow spiritually?

Chapter 10

My personal beliefs

❖

My desire is for this book to be accessible to all leaders who are interested in personal development and growth and who want to make a more meaningful impact in the world.

While writing this book, I have specifically been mindful of my own beliefs, limitations and convictions. As mentioned in Chapter 1, I do hold a specific worldview, which shapes how I see life and the topic of leadership.

I want this book to convey what I have experienced through the eyes of exceptional leaders as well as my own experiences and reflections. I want to share what I have learnt and am still learning. For me, it is a journey of grace, in other words, not one characterised by some supposedly special individual quality but one marked by unmerited favour that has been extended to me.

Even if you believe very differently from me, I trust that you have gotten this far in this book because we have something in common: we believe the world can and should be a better place for all people. We want a world where all human beings can live without hunger, poverty or abuse with dignity and respected as equal in value.

From our privileged position as organisational leaders, it is easy to forget others. Living in Africa, I often see mansions and small shacks within minutes of each other, and I wonder how this can continue to be the norm.

What I hope you and I have in common is that a significant part of our purpose is to help create that better world. For me, that conviction has a spiritual source. For you, it might be that conviction which leads you to your spiritual Source.

I encourage leaders to be open and honest yet humble about their worldviews, beliefs and spiritual practices. This chapter is my attempt to practice what I preach. Although you may agree or disagree with my personal beliefs, which undoubtedly influenced the framework I present in this book, I encourage you to consider it all with an open mind and spirit. Regardless of whether you disagree with me on any specific aspect, my hope is that it opens the way for you to share your views, with me or those in your world, with deep love and care.

I have already shared aspects of my leadership journey with you. I started my career as a warden working in South Africa's prison system. This is where I started studying to become an industrial psychologist. I am currently an executive leadership coach and facilitator, and I run my business in cooperation with several other talented and inspiring leaders. My work offers me the privilege to work with gifted, experienced and principled leaders from across the globe.

In my years as an executive coach, I cannot remember one instance where someone who I coached challenged or asked me what I stand for or what my inner source is. I find it surprising that we allow others to influence who we are unconditionally, without understanding who they are. Many people accept the input of thought leaders or experts without questioning.

I suggest that we should interrogate the sources of those from whom we receive input. I have taken the time to explore what the inner sources of great thought leaders like Freud, Darwin and Jung were to decide if I wanted to follow their thinking. I found, for example, that Freud viewed people as only consisting of a soul and a body with no spirit.[52] I believe that this view has made us as humans spiritually poorer, so I am cautious of putting too much credit in Freud's theories.

In light of this principle, I would like to share more about my worldview and my Source with you. As you know by now, though, I am very sceptical of labels, so allow me to describe my beliefs to you rather than to summarise it with a label.

My conviction is that there is a deep yearning in our spirits to be connected to the Spirit of God. This yearning encapsulates our ultimate concern and purpose as people. It is the wellspring from where we seek and find the worthy goals in life that go beyond personal gain.

I used the neutral term "Source" in this book to make the content as widely accessible and valuable as possible. For me, however, the term "Spirit of God" does far more justice to my spiritual experiences than referring to a "Source". The Spirit of God is my Source, but this Source is not an abstract concept. It is a Being with whom I have a personal relationship, even though this relationship, like God, is far more than any connection I can have with another person. My spirit is only strong while in a relationship with the Spirit of God.

I know there are different spiritual dimensions, and different people have different spiritual experiences. However, sometimes when people use phrases like "the universe" or "our God-Self", I get the sense that they use it without fully understanding what they are talking about. When I ask them what they really mean, they are not able to describe it clearly and in a meaningful way. They might not want to offend me or anyone else, or they might not know what they mean and what they believe.

I believe we should take a stance in love and talk about what we really believe. We need spaces where we can be safe enough but also brave enough to examine what we believe and share it with each other.

My view is that the human spirit that is not connected to the Spirit of God becomes a super spirit. Like a super soul, this person's spirit may be very spiritually aware, but it does not reach its ultimate purpose, which is relationship with God's Spirit. That said, every person must get their own clarity on the nature and state of their spiritual self and how they have access to the Spirit of God.

It is in relationship with the Spirit of God that I have discovered my spiritual self as the wellspring of life. Even if I sometimes have to dig deep to get guidance and clarity, God's Spirit is my source of spiritual wisdom that assists me in all spheres of life. I have found it very important to develop my connection with the Spirit of God through daily reflection, prayer, meditation and listening. When I intentionally work on it daily, it gives me the ability to instinctively draw from this relationship in an instant during a crisis.

I have found that my relationship with the Spirit of God produces fruits and gifts that are available to me and those around me. Love, peace, freedom and joy are spiritual fruit that have grown my character. I even experience spiritual gifts and anointing which go beyond what we can understand with our rational minds because of grace and my relationship with the Spirit of God. However, these things come because of constant hard work. It is not a once-off achievement. Any person, no matter how spiritually advanced, can fail in a second.

To me, the result of a life in the Spirit cannot be anything else but the marks of the Spirit: love, joy, peace, patience, kindness, goodness, faithfulness, gentleness and self-control, as it is described in the *Bible* in Galatians 5:22-23. It is interesting to me that there is no sense of urgency or personal ambition in these characteristics. They highlight a different and more appropriate approach to leading people in the world of work, including a more humane work environment.

As a leader, I continually strive to engage my spirit intentionally – personally and in my work. I am not aware of a better option of how to navigate our complex global system. It gives me clarity of personal passion, purpose and freedom, imbued with love. It has become a spiritual blueprint for living out my unique vision.

Whatever your story might be, I encourage you to continue with the journey sparked by your conviction that we as leaders can make the world a better place. As leaders in all spheres of society, let us show others how they can embark on this journey too, especially as it relates to the things that matter most.

Continue to develop as a person and a leader. Continue to foster and cherish relationships with others. And continue seeking your Source until you find it in all its fullness. Have conversations about your spirit. Dig deep and get clarity on what it means to you. Find that thing which will fill the void inside of you and give your life ultimate meaning.

My research has confirmed what I have experienced and felt in my heart. This life and spiritual journey that I describe above – even though it is often an enigma and we only know things in part – is the way to make a meaningful impact and create a better world for all of us.

I invite you to embark on this journey and to continue with it, no matter the obstacles or costs.

As Antoine de Saint-Exupéry says in *The Little Prince*, "It is only with the heart that one sees rightly; what is essential is invisible to the eye".[53]

Conclusion

❖

So, how do we navigate the complexity of our interconnected global system and the tensions of international, regional and internal organisational conflict to lead towards a better future with purpose and integrity?

The answer, as the title of this book suggests, is our inner source, of course.

The seven leadership dimensions that my PhD research uncovered and that make up the bulk of this book is a framework to help guide us along the way and keep us connected to our source.

They are not simplistic tactics, though. For instance, very few situations would require that you only apply one. In fact, as you might have gathered from the examples in each chapter, the lines between the dimensions can often get blurry. Together, they describe an approach to leadership that is not easy or simple, but deeply rewarding for ambitious, principled leaders who want to make a positive impact in the world.

Two metaphors for this framework that come to mind is a piece of cloth with interwoven strands of fabric made of different colours. The colours don't always remain distinct, but that unity contributes to the beauty and the utility of the cloth to undergird you.

You can also think of the framework as a beacon of light that illuminates your path and shows you where to go. It is not the goal of your leadership journey or even the end destination. The purpose of this framework is not to tell you what to do during every single moment – it's to help you figure out your own unique path, complete with bumps and bruises. And it will likely be most useful to you during the darkest times when you're closest to veering off this path of light.

Each of our leadership journeys are unique. I have used the characters of Prathiba, Sibu and Hugo as well as stories from my own life and that of my clients as illustrations. It might be that you have gleaned something from those stories, but more likely than not, you won't find the answers for your toughest leadership challenges in the experience of someone else. You will have to forge the path for yourself.

That is why I have encouraged you to reflect at the end of each chapter on what that information means to you. What resonated for you? How will you apply it? What will you do differently?

However, reflection by itself is usually not enough to result in breakthrough growth. When we work on our own, we tend to find confirmation for what we already believe. To see things in new ways, we often need to allow others to challenge our thinking.

Yes, you certainly can be challenged by reading a book. However, the fastest way to personal insight and breakthrough is in conversation with someone you trust and who cares enough about you to challenge you.

As a leader, you're likely great at bringing out in others what they can't see in themselves. But as a leader, the chances of someone doing that for you during the normal course of the day get less. You need to consciously create circumstances that are conducive to growth if you don't want to stagnate. Because, as Marshall Goldsmith's book title puts it, *What Got You Here Won't Get You There.*

At the end of this book, I'd therefore like to challenge you: get someone else involved in your leadership journey.

If you already have a trusted mentor or coach, share your takeaways and insights from this book with them.

If you do not have such a person, think of someone who genuinely cares about your growth, will ask you hard questions and keep you accountable. Make an appointment with them to ask whether they would be willing to fulfil the role of sounding board and accountability partner in your life.

Since these people are likely not professional coaches, as a bonus, I share a structured approach that you and the person you trust can use to develop a personal leadership action plan for yourself. I've used similar approaches with my clients, so I know this approach works. It's not complicated, but it forces you to reflect on the most important things and to keep accountable.

I believe in you. The fact that you have read this book tells me that you have the desire to be and do more, and that is the catalyst for meaningful growth and impact.

I wish you all the best in your leadership journey, and I look forward to if and when our paths may cross again after this book.

Your Personal Leadership Action Plan

❖

To get a free electronic copy of this plan as an editable Microsoft Word document, go to: https://kr.co.za/The-Leaders-Inner-Source-Coaching-Action-Plan

My leadership slogan/life theme *(keep it short and to the point)*:

NAME:_____ **Date last updated:** _____

People who will support me on this journey:

- Family:

- Friends:

- Colleagues and leaders who will support me:

- Colleagues and leaders who believe in me at all costs:

My vision:	
My personal aspirations:	1. 2. 3.
My professional aspirations:	1. 2. 3.

My biggest opportunity:	
My key strengths (refer to assessments, 360 feedback, etc.):	1. 2. 3.
My areas for growth (refer to assessments, 360 feedback, etc.):	1. 2. 3.
My short-term goals (1 to 2 years): Body: Intellectual: Emotional: Spiritual: Family (relationships): Social (relationships): Career (business relationships):	

My medium-term goals (3 to 5 years): Body: Intellectual: Emotional: Spiritual: Family (relationships): Social (relationships): Career (business relationships):		
MY FOCUS NOW		
Goal 1:		
My motivation	**What is the value of achieving this goal?**	
My current situations	**How would you rate your competence in this area now?** **High Medium Low Non-existent**	
Planning and actions	**What needs to be actioned to achieve this goal?**	
Progress	Date:	Not Achieved
	Date:	Partially Achieved
	Date:	Mostly Achieved
	Date:	Achieved
	Date:	Exceeded
REFLECTION AND DEVELOPMENT:	**What learning has happened to date regarding this goal?** **What changes am I making using this learning?**	

MY FOCUS NOW		
Goal 2:		
My motivation	**What is the value of achieving this goal?**	
My current situations	**How would you rate your competence in this area now?** **High Medium Low Non-existent**	
Planning and actions	**What needs to be actioned to achieve this goal?**	
Progress	Date:	Not Achieved
	Date:	Partially Achieved
	Date:	Mostly Achieved
	Date:	Achieved
	Date:	Exceeded
REFLECTION AND DEVELOPMENT:	**What learning has happened to date regarding this goal?** **What changes am I making using this learning?**	
MY FOCUS NOW		
Goal 3:		
My motivation	**What is the value of achieving this goal?**	
My current situations	**How would you rate your competence in this area now?** **High Medium Low Non-existent**	
Planning and actions	**What needs to be actioned to achieve this goal?**	
Progress	Date:	Not Achieved

	Date:	Partially Achieved
	Date:	Mostly Achieved
	Date:	Achieved
	Date:	Exceeded
REFLECTION AND DEVELOPMENT	**What learning has happened to date regarding this goal?** **What changes am I making using this learning?**	

References

❖

Achor, S., Reece, A., Kellerman, G.R. and Robichaux, A. 2018. 9 Out of 10 People Are Willing to Earn Less Money to Do More-Meaningful Work. *Harvard Business Review*. 6 November. Available at https://hbr.org/2018/11/9-out-of-10-people-are-willing-to-earn-less-money-to-do-more-meaningful-work

Anderson, B. 1993. *Leadership: Uncommon Sense*. Available at http://www.leadershipcircle.com

AZ Quotes. n.d. C Northcote Parkinson quotes. Available at: https://www.azquotes.com/author/11333-C_Northcote_Parkinson

Blanchard, K. 2006. *The Leadership Summit of Self-leadership* Audio CD. 1 January. Willow Creek Association.

Brown, B. 2010. *The Power of Vulnerability*. TED talk. Available at https://www.ted.com/talks/brene_brown_the_power_of_vulnerability

Burke, A. 2007. *Nurturing the Spirit*. Basic seminar. Amethyst Healing: Sapphire Leadership Group.

Clifton, J. 2021. *Gallup Finds a Silver Bullet: Coach Me Once Per Week*. Gallup. 27 May. Available at https://www.gallup.com/workplace/350057/gallup-finds-silver-bullet-coach-once-per-week.aspx

Croom, S. 2021. *12% of corporate leaders are psychopaths. It's time to take this problem seriously*. Fortune. 6 June. Available at https://fortune.com/2021/06/06/corporate-psychopaths-business-leadership-csr/

Cunningham, L.A. 1997. *The Essays of Warren Buffett: Lessons for Corporate America*. Cardozo Law Review.

De Saint-Exupéry, A. 1943. *The Little Prince*. Reynal & Hitchcock.

Du Plessis, R. 2015. *The Spiritual Self of the Corporate Leader*. PhD Thesis, The Da Vinci Institute for Technology Management.

Edelman Trust Barometer. (2009). *Global opinion leaders study*. Produced by Research Firm, StrategyOne. Available at www.edelmaneditions.com

Edelman Trust Barometer. (2012). *Global opinion leaders study*. Produced by Research Firm, StrategyOne. Available at www.edelmaneditions.com

Edelman Trust Barometer. (2023). *Global opinion leaders study*. Produced by Research Firm, StrategyOne. Available at www.edelmaneditions.com

Ferrazzi, K. 2005. *Never Eat Alone: And Other Secrets to Success, One Relationship at a Time*. With Tahl Raz. Crown Business.

Fry, L.W. 2008. *Spiritual Leadership as an Integrating Paradigm for Positive Leadership Development*. Presentation obtained from SASOL, South Africa.

Fry, L.W. 2009. *Maximizing the Triple Bottom Line and Spiritual Leadership: The CEL Story*. Presented at the Academy of Management Meeting, Chicago, Illinois.

Grant, L. 2010. Your Most Important Business Asset: Relationships. Nasdaq. 27 October. Available at https://www.nasdaq.com/articles/your-most-important-business-asset%3A-relationships-2010-10-27

International Centre for Spirit at Work (ICSW). 2011. *The 2008 International Spirit at Work Award*. Available at www.spiritatwork.org

Kahneman, D. 2011. *Thinking, Fast and Slow*. Farrar, Straus and Giroux.

Kahneman, D., Sibony, O, & Sustain, C.R. 2021. *Noise*. Harper Collins Publishers, Ireland.

Kurtz, C.F. & Snowden, D.J. 2003. The New Dynamics of Strategy: Sense-making in a Complex-Complicated World. *IBM Systems Journal,* 42(3): 462-483.

Leaf, C. 2013. *Switch on Your Brain: The Key to Peak Happiness, Thinking and Health*. Baker Books.

Lambourne, W. 2012. *Legitimate Leadership*. CreateSpace Independent Publishing Platform.

Mandelbrot, B.B. 2004. *Fractals and Chaos. The Mandelbrot Set and Beyond*. Springer.

Maslow, A. 1943. A Theory of Human Motivation. *Psychological Review,* 50(4), 370-396.

Mathews, D.A., Larson, D.B. & Barry, C.P. 1994. *The Faith Factor: An Annotated Bibliography of Clinical Research on Spiritual Subjects*. John Templeton Foundation, National Institute for Healthcare Research.

Norden, N. 2015. *God Speaks! Listen*. Living Word, Pretoria.

Parikh, J. 1994. *Managing Your Self: Management by Detached Involvement*. Blackwell Publishers.

Peacocke, D. 2003. *Doing Business God's Way*. Rebuild.

Prinsloo, M. 2020. *Written communication between the author and Marelize Prinsloo, Managing Director of Cognadev, about research conducted by Cognadev*. 8 May. Company website available at https://www.cognadev.com/

PWC. 2016. *19ᵗʰ Annual Global CEO Survey*. Available at www.pwc.com/ceosurvey

Rath, T. 2007. *StrengthsFinder 2.0*. Gallup Press.

Royal, K. 2019. *What Engaged Employees Do Differently*. Gallup Workplace. 14 September. Available at https://www.gallup.com/workplace/266822/engaged-employees-differently.aspx

Ryff, C.D. & Singer, B.H. 2001. *New Horizons in Health*. Washington, DC: National Research Council National Academies Press.

Scharmer, O. 2007. *Theory U: Leading from the Future as It Emerges*. Society of Organisational Learning.

Sharma, R.S. 2004. *The Monk Who Sold His Ferrari*. Harper Collins.

Squires, A., Wade, J., Dominick, P., & Gelosh, D. 2011. *Building a Competency Taxonomy to Guide Experience Acceleration of Lead Program Systems Engineers*. In 9th Annual Conference on Systems Engineering Research (CSER) (pp. 1–10). Redondo Beach, CA

Taleb, N. 2007. *The Black Swan: The Impact of the Highly Improbably*. Random House.

Van der Westhuizen, J. 2020. *Telephonic interview between the author and Jan van der Westhuizen, Managing Director of Experttech*. Company website available at https://www.expert-tech.co.za/

Vargas, R.V., Oumarou, T.A & Andersson, E. 2021. *Transformation is personal*. Business Review. 12 January. Available at https://blogs.lse.ac.uk/businessreview/2021/01/12/transformation-is-personal/#:~:text=Individual%20transformation%20of%20employees%20is,changes%20are%20almost%20non%2Dexistent

Wheatley, M.J. 2005. *Finding Our Way: Leadership for Uncertain Times*. Berrett-Koehler.

Zak, P.J. 2017. The Neuroscience of Trust. *Harvard Business Review*. January/February. Available at https://hbr.org/2017/01/the-neuroscience-of-trust

Zellers, K.L. & Perrewe, P.L. 2003. *Handbook of Workplace Spirituality and Organisational Performance*. In R.A. Giacalone and C.L. Jurkiewicz (Eds.), (300-313). ME Sharp.

Zimbardo, P.G. 2007. *The Lucifer Effect: Understanding How Good People Turn Evil*. Random House.

Endnotes

❖

1   Taleb, 2007.
2   Edelman Trust Barometer, 2023:11.
3   Edelman Trust Barometer, 2009:1-3.
4   Gallup, 2022.
5   Achor et al., 2018.
6   Gallup, 2022:6.
7   Royal, 2019.
8   Zak, 2017.
9   Gallup, 2023:4.
10 Scharmer, 2007.
11 Du Plessis, 2015.
12 Squires, Wade, Dominick & Gelosh, 2011.
13 Kurtz & Snowden, 2003.
14 Prinsloo, 2020.
15 Van der Westhuizen, 2020.
16 Prinsloo, 2020.
17 Kahneman, 2011.
18 Kahneman, Sibony & Sustain, 2021.
19 Mandelbrot, 2004.
20 Croom, 2021.
21 Parkinson, n.d.
22 Anderson, 1993.
23 Vargas, Oumarou & Andersson, 2021.
24 Norden, 2015:6.
25 Burke, 2007.
26 Leaf, 2013.
27 Wheatley, 2005:21, 28.
28 Rath, 2007:i.
29 Sharma, 2004.
30 Cunningham, 1997.
31 Parikh, 1994:25.
32 Lambourne, 2012:24
33 Lambourne, 2012:17.
34 Parikh, 1994.
35 Parikh, 1994:28.
36 Brown, 2010.
37 Gallup, 2023.
38 Clifton, 2021.
39 Clifton, 2021.

40   Clifton, 2021.
41   Lambourne, 2012:26.
42   Lambourne, 2012:72.
43   Lambourne, 2012:163.
44   Maslow, 1943.
45   Blanchard, 2006.
46   Ferrazzi, 2005.
47   Grant, 2010.
48   Zimbardo, 2007:460.
49   ICSW, 2011.
50   Du Plessis, 2015.
51   Mathews, Larson & Barry, 1994; Zellers & Perrewe, 2003; Fry, 2008; 2009; Ryff & Singer, 2001.
52   Peacocke, 2003:108.
53   Saint-Exupéry, 1943.

Index

❖

T

thoughts, words and actions,
80
tripartite self, 41–42, 120

U

unconditional engagement, 12,
48, 92, 94–96, 98–102

W

western worldview, 37–40, 52,
120
worldviews, 35–37, 39–41, 45,
78, 98, 132

www.ingramcontent.com/pod-product-compliance
Lightning Source LLC
Chambersburg PA
CBHW071840200326
41519CB00016B/4188